CATHOLICISM.

THE PIVOTAL PLAYERS

VOLUME I

Dear Friends,

To be holy is to be like Christ. The call to holiness is universal, which means that holiness is not meant for only a privileged few, but it is the mission towards which all Christ's disciples should aspire. Those who aspire to holiness will become for others a way of knowing Christ, for Christ introduces himself to the world, not merely in abstractions or emotions or institutions, but through the people he has called to be his friends. As such, the presence of Christ is embodied in the lives of real people, in men and women who know Christ and through lives made distinct by their relationship with Christ, seek to introduce him to the world.

The saints are exemplars of holiness par excellence. In their lives the form of Christ takes shape and becomes tangible to the world. The world will experience in the saint a person, who like Christ, is both ordinary and extraordinary. To encounter a saint is to experience the natural as imbued with the supernatural, virtues are elevated by divine grace, and human weakness is overcome by an uncanny strength. The saint becomes for the Church and the world an exemplification of what holiness really and truly means, and from their witness all disciples discern their own call to holiness.

Not all who know Christ will manifest the heroic virtue that makes one a saint, but all Christians are gifted with the potential for mighty deeds and can contribute, in accord with their state of life, to the transformation of all things in Christ. For some, this work of transformation will reveal itself to the world in readily apparent ways, and for others it will remain hidden, but whether apparent or hidden, it is Christ who is present, active, and working.

CATHOLICISM: *The Pivotal Players* Volume One has been created as a tribute to those men and women whose friendship with Christ transformed not only their own lives, but also the world. I have envisioned this new series as a continuation of the original CATHOLICISM series and a complement to CATHOLICISM: *The New Evangelization.* Whereas the CATHOLICISM series presented the rich content of the Church's Faith, and CATHOLICISM: *The New Evangelization* insisted that the Church's Faith is always a public act of introduction to Christ, CATHOLICISM: *The Pivotal Players* displays the potential that friendship with Christ unleashes in the lives of his disciples. It is my hope that those who view CATHOLICISM: *The Pivotal Players* will discover in these men and women not just people to be admired, but an invitation to accept as their own the universal call to holiness.

Peace,

+ Robert Barron

Bishop Robert Barron
Founder, Word on Fire
Auxiliary Bishop of Los Angeles

WORD on FIRE

CATHOLICISM

THE PIVOTAL PLAYERS

VOLUME I

Leader Guide

BASED ON THE SERIES CREATED BY

Bishop Robert Barron

AUTHORS

*Fr. Raniero Cantalamessa, Dr. Matthew Levering, Fr. Paul Murray, O.P.,
Fr. Ian Ker, Dale Ahlquist, Dr. Anthony M. Esolen*

Facilitator Guide and Answer Key written by Peggy Pandaleon

FACILITATOR GUIDE

CATHOLICISM

THE PIVOTAL PLAYERS

VOLUME I

Facilitator Guide written by Peggy Pandaleon

CATHOLICISM
THE PIVOTAL PLAYERS
Facilitator Guide

STUDY PROGRAM CHECKLIST

This is a summary of all the key steps Word on Fire recommends for the *CATHOLICISM: The Pivotal Players* Formation Program. You can use it in your planning and program administration. Additional detail for each phase is provided in the remainder of this guide.

PHASE ONE: PLANNING

☐ **PRAY** your way through all planning and put your trust in the Holy Spirit. As St. Paul tells us in First Thessalonians, "Rejoice always. Pray without ceasing."

☐ At least three months before you launch the program, the Program Coordinator should **meet with the Pastor or Group Director** to secure approval and to plan the dates of the program, including the pre-program Leader's Orientation session.

☐ Identify and **reserve the place** where the program will be held. This room should include:

- DVD or Blu-ray player with a screen large enough to be viewed by the entire class. If you have a big group, it is often helpful to have the screen raised for easier viewing
- Chairs to accommodate all participants
- Break-out rooms or secluded areas for small group discussion— a separate space for each group (Many participants enjoy gathering around tables for discussion so they can spread out their materials.)

☐ **Recruit other members** of the leadership team, namely the Program Administrator and Group Discussion Leaders. You should have one Group Leader for every 8-10 people.

☐ **Order the Study Program Leader's Kit** about two months ahead, so the Program Coordinator can review the materials and begin to plan the Leaders' Orientation session.

☐ Determine if the **cost of the program materials** will be passed through to the participants. Don't forget to include shipping, handling, applicable tax, and any other expenses your program will incur in the total cost to be allocated and assigned as a registration fee. Don't hesitate to charge a registration fee as people often value something more if they have to pay for it.

☐ **Publicize the *CATHOLICISM: The Pivotal Players* program** with free, downloadable posters and flyers found at *pivotalplayers.wordonfire.org/#support*

☐ Place an **announcement in the Sunday bulletin** that includes a registration form (available at *pivotalplayers.wordonfire.org/#support*). Ask for the registration form and fee to be submitted at least three weeks ahead of the start of the program so you can order the right number of Study Guides for your group. We suggest ordering a few extra knowing that you can return them within 90 days for a full refund, if they have not been unwrapped.

☐ Plan at least one Sunday where the program can be **announced from the pulpit**. Set up a registration table in the vestibule staffed by the leadership team and complete with registration forms and a sample study guide. If possible, play the *CATHOLICISM: The Pivotal Players* trailer on a laptop, so parishioners can experience the visual impact of the study. The trailer can be found at: *pivotalplayers.wordonfire.org/#watch*

☐ Right before the Leaders' Orientation Session, the Program Administrator should **compile a roster** of all registrants that includes contact information.

☐ **Assign each participant on the roster to a Group Discussion Leader** (to be announced at Leaders' Orientation). Try to balance age, gender, and adult formation experience, so each group has a diverse mix. Also, if you know many of the registrants, try to balance the "talkers" with the "listeners."

☐ Hold the **Group Leaders' Orientation Session** one to two weeks ahead of the start of the program. See details in the Leadership Preparation section on page 11.

PHASE 2: HOSTING THE PROGRAM

☐ **PRAY** your way through the program and put your trust in the Holy Spirit. As St. Paul tells us in First Thessalonians, "Rejoice always. Pray without ceasing."

☐ **First session:** *Welcome and Orientation.* Create an atmosphere where people can comfortably orient themselves to the program and get to know their small groups.

☐ **Begin Leadership Prep Meetings** before the second session. Meet to pray, review *Questions for Understanding* and discuss any administrative issues.

☐ Make sure there is **a way for participants to ask questions** that might remain after the group discussion. If you have a priest or deacon involved, questions may be directed to him. If you do not have access to a priest, you can send unanswered questions to *StudyPrograms@wordonfire.org* and a member of the Word on Fire team will respond.

☐ **Encourage the Group Leaders to contact each of their group members** regularly outside of the program session. Group leaders can call, email, or connect with participants in person. This contact is important to build fellowship among the small groups, to uncover any concerns, and to promote trust and openness. Remember, evangelization starts with a loving *relationship*.

PHASE 3: EVALUATION AND NEXT STEPS

☐   **PRAY** your way through evaluation and put your trust in the Holy Spirit. As St. Paul tells us in First Thessalonians, "Rejoice always. Pray without ceasing."

☐   Revise and/or hand out the survey (found at *pivotalplayers.wordonfire.org/#support*) a few sessions before the program ends. Encourage all participants and leaders to complete the survey, so you can continually improve your Adult Formation ministry.

☐   Share any comments or suggestions with Word on Fire by emailing: **StudyPrograms@wordonfire.org**

☐   Discuss options for your next Adult Formation Program. Word on Fire offers other study programs based on Bishop Barron's videos. For more information on these programs, visit *www.WordOnFire.org/Study-Programs/*.

STUDY PROGRAM MATERIALS

Everyone will need to have a Catholic translation of the Bible and access to the *Catechism of the Catholic Church* to complete the questions in each lesson. Catholic translations include:

- *Revised Standard Version:* A more literal translation used for serious Scripture study
- *New American Bible:* Used in the liturgy and is easier to read
- *New Jerusalem Bible:* More contemporary language, but still true to the original meaning

To look up references in the *Catechism of the Catholic Church*, you can purchase a copy of the *Catechism* or go to this website and enter the paragraph number to display the text: *www.scborromeo.org/ccc.htm*

Each person must have his or her own Study Guide so everyone can write answers to the questions and take notes individually. The copying of lessons, without permission, is strictly forbidden by copyright laws.

It is suggested that you order the Leader's Guide for each small Group Discussion Leader as it contains the Facilitator Guide and Answer Key.

Every lesson follows the same format:
    <u>Outline</u>: Summarizes the video presentation and is useful for taking notes while watching

    <u>Commentary</u>: Expands on and captures much of the content presented in the video. Contains all the information needed to answer the *Questions for Understanding*.

    Questions for Understanding: Answers can be found in the film lesson and commentary primarily, with some reference to the Bible and the *Catechism of the Catholic Church*. Participants should be encouraged to write down their answers, as research shows that the simple act of writing something down significantly increases retention. Each discussion session should cover all of the *Questions for Understanding*, so please budget your time accordingly.

    Questions for Application: Each discussion should include **at least two** *Questions for Application*. Group leaders can assign specific questions the week before, so participants can prepare those that will be discussed. If some of the questions seem too personal, please still encourage your participants to reflect on and pray about them privately. The Study Program provides many opportunities for each participant's spiritual enrichment, whether in a group or individually.

    <u>Endnotes</u>: Provided at the end of some lessons. The Endnotes provide some references for material cited in the commentary.

Additional materials included in the Leader's Kit can be used to enrich and supplement the videos and Study Guides. These additional materials include:

Praying with the Pivotal Players by Amy Welborn

One copy of this book is included to support prayer within the program and also to provide additional information about the Pivotal Players' lives for the program leadership. Additional copies of this book can be purchased at: _http://www.wordonfire.org/resources/book/pre-order-praying-with-the-pivotal-players/5188/_

Pivotal Players Prayer Card Packet

The _Pivotal Players_ Prayer Card Packet contains 120 prayer cards. Each card contains the same prayer written especially for this program, plus an original image of one of the Pivotal Players. You can use these cards to build awareness of the Pivotal Players Study Program and/or to pray during the study program sessions. It will be easy for participants to pray along, if they each have a prayer card. Additional Prayer Card Packets can be purchased at: _http://www.wordonfire.org/resources/misc/pre-order-catholicism-the-pivotal-players---prayer-card-packet/5192/_

Pivotal Players Answer Key

Provided for the group facilitator, this resource gives an in-depth answer to each _Question for Understanding_. It is not intended to be a "black-and-white, right-or-wrong" checklist against which all participants' responses are judged. Therefore, please be cautious when sharing this information, as some may become discouraged if they perceive that they should produce the same answer.

PROGRAM PLANNING

1. Set up the dates and times for the program according to procedures in your parish or group. Make sure to discuss the program plans with your pastor or group leader.

    It is helpful to publish a complete calendar for the program that includes each session's date and what will be covered in that session. The session schedule for each program option is listed in the Program Structure section, beginning on page 15.

2. Assemble your Leadership Team (see below).

3. Announce the program to the parish or group. Free materials are available at *pivotalplayers.wordonfire. org/#support*. These include: flyers, posters, bulletin and pulpit announcements, and registration forms.

4. Strive to have one Sunday set aside where the program can be announced from the pulpit at all Masses, and parishioners can register as they exit the church.

    Set up a table in the vestibule and have the Study Guide there for review and registration forms available. If possible, run the *CATHOLICISM: The Pivotal Players* trailer on a laptop, so parishioners can experience the visual impact of the study. The trailer can be found at *pivotalplayers.wordonfire.org/#watch*

5. Run an announcement in the Sunday bulletin, which should include a registration form that specifies the registration fee. The fee should cover the purchase of a Study Guide for each participant plus any other program expenses that you want to pass through to them. Provide a deadline for registration that is at least three weeks before your first session, so you can order a Study Guide for each participant. You might want to order a few more than you think you will need as most groups have walk-in participants at the first session. Study Guides can be returned within 90 days of purchase for a full refund if they are not used or unwrapped.

6. Supply and collect registration forms, so you know how many will participate and can order the right number of Study Guides. Most parishes charge a registration fee that covers the Study Guides and other materials as necessary. It's human nature to value what you pay for more than something that is free, so don't hesitate to charge for the program. A registration form template can be downloaded at *http://pivotalplayers.wordonfire.org/#support*

LEADERSHIP TEAM

The three key roles on the Leadership Team are:

- Program Coordinator
- Program Administrator
- Group Discussion Leader

PROGRAM COORDINATOR:

- Manages the overall program and is the key contact for the pastor and parish
- Plans and executes the promotion of the study program
- Begins each session with prayer and announcements when all are assembled as a group
- Recruits Group Discussion Leaders with the approval of the pastor or supervisor of the community
- Addresses issues and concerns of participants if they arise

PROGRAM ADMINISTRATOR:

- Manages the registration process, including finances for the group
- Orders and distributes materials
- Develops a roster that lists all participants and their contact information
- Makes nametags for each participant and Group Leader

GROUP DISCUSSION LEADER:

- Leads a group of 8-10 participants
- Takes attendance each session and contacts members who miss frequently to discern if issues are present
- Facilitates discussion of lesson questions, committing to complete all *Questions for Understanding* and two *Questions for Application*
- Can also serve as Program Coordinator and/or Administrator

LEADERSHIP PREPARATION

A few weeks before the start of your *Pivotal Players* program, plan to host a **Leaders' Orientation Session**. This can be accomplished in about two hours and should include the following:

Prayer and Spiritual Enrichment: Invite a priest or experienced speaker to lead a 45-60 minute spiritual enrichment session. This could be on any facet of the Church and should include some assigned reading from Scripture or specific writings. The purpose of this time is to grow spiritually and prepare for the mission of adult formation and evangelization.

Program Overview: Explain the structure of the *Pivotal Players* program, including the leadership meetings before each session and the unique activities that will be part of the Orientation Session. Give each leader his/her own Leader's Guide, which contains this Facilitator Guide, all the lessons and the Answer Key. Ask the leadership team to briefly review the materials before the program starts.

Group Leader's Role: Review the section of this guide that explains the role of a Group Discussion Leader when you are together at this meeting. Reinforce that the leader is a *facilitator*, not a teacher or expert.

Group Assignment: Give each leader a list of his or her members and their contact information. Word on Fire suggests that you pre-assign groups, so friends and spouses do not sit together. It is important that each member comes to their discussion group as an individual and forms new bonds within this group. Pre-existing relationships have certain communication patterns and "inside connections" that could create a clique-like atmosphere, which will work against group cohesion.

Once the groups are assigned, ask each leader to contact his or her members for a friendly introduction and to provide a reminder about the first session's date and time.

Administrative Tasks: You can enlist your leadership team to help with tasks that are necessary to prepare for the first session (e.g., making name tags; unpacking study guides; preparing "get to know you" exercises for the first session, etc.)

Leadership Prep Meeting Planning: Begin regular preparation meetings with the leadership team before the second session. This meeting should be held before each of the twelve general sessions to pray together and also to help the Group Discussion Leaders prepare to facilitate their groups by going through the *Questions for Understanding* together.

During each Leadership Prep meeting (60-75 minutes) plan to:

1. **Pray as a team** for the program as a whole and for any individual intentions. These meetings should begin and end with prayer. Often, the leadership team will bring the needs of individuals in their small groups to prayer at these meetings.

2. **Review** the *Questions for Understanding*. When the Leaders spend some time discussing their own responses and all the resources they uncovered to answer the questions, they will be much better prepared to facilitate their own small groups.

3. **Discuss** any administrative or participant issues.

GROUP LEADER GUIDELINES

Role:

<u>You are Christ's representative to your small group</u>. As a Leader, people will look to you to model Christ's attitudes and behavior and to also be loyal and true to the teachings of his Church. During the study, enrich your own spiritual life by spending more time in prayer, attending Mass more frequently, and receiving the Sacraments regularly.

<u>You are a facilitator, not a teacher or expert</u>. You are called to facilitate discussion of the study guide questions in the small groups, not to teach the material or give your own answers to the questions. Use the resources provided in the Leader's Kit, especially the Study Guide Commentary and the Answer Key, to guide your group to more fully understand the content of each lesson. The philosophy of this approach is that we are all adults learning together with Bishop Barron as our "teacher," under the guidance of the Holy Spirit. Group Leaders facilitate this learning without becoming experts or teachers themselves. If there are outstanding questions at the end of the group discussion, you should first seek out a priest or deacon for guidance. In addition, Word on Fire can help with questions when emailed to **StudyPrograms@WordOnFire.org**

<u>You are the shepherd of the group</u>. Help each member feel comfortable. Keep discussion focused on the material for that lesson. Lead with love and a positive attitude of acceptance of each person's worth in Christ.

Your goal is to create and maintain positive group dynamics in the discussion. Some groups may have one or more challenging people that you will have to manage within the group discussion or talk to privately. Please review *Managing Personalities* in the Support Materials section at *http://pivotalplayers.wordonfire.org/#support*

Responsibilities:

1. Outside of class time, **pray for your group** collectively and as individuals. Also, before beginning the discussion of the lesson, say a short prayer with the group.

2. **Be watchful for "contrary spirits."** Increase your own prayer time and reception of the Sacraments, especially the Eucharist, to access God's grace to fortify your leadership.

3. **Create a relaxed, warm atmosphere of acceptance and eagerness to learn from one another.**

- Get to know your members. Contact them outside of class two or three times during the program to build relationships and answer any questions they may have.
- Maintain eye contact in the group.
- Reassure that "we are all learning together."
- Encourage the use of name tags.

4. **Establish that you are the facilitator and leader of the discussion.**

- If your group is assembled around a table, sit at the head of the table and block the other head, if there is one. If seated at a round table or in a circle of chairs, sit in the chair facing the door and leave the spot opposite you open (i.e., in a horseshoe-type pattern)
- If possible, face the door so you can welcome late-comers
- To ensure positive group dynamics, manage personalities within the group or by talking to the person privately. Some helpful tips can be found in the *Managing Personalities* summary in the Support Materials section at *pivotalplayers.wordonfire.org/#support*

5. **Act as a facilitator, not as a teacher or expert.**

- <u>Draw answers from your group; refrain from teaching</u>. Refrain from teaching or sharing your own opinions and answers to the questions. Remain neutral as much as possible, so members feel they can express differing thoughts and not look for the Leader's answer as affirmation. Be patient when there is silence. Don't jump in with answers, but you can rephrase the question or ask probing questions to foster dialogue.

- <u>Use discernment in handling misconceptions</u>. Try to tactfully bring out the truth according to the Church's teaching. It is useful to ask for other opinions among the group if an answer seems confusing or does not reflect the truth of God's word.

- <u>Keep track of time</u>, Lessons should be completed during your allotted time. Avoid getting off the subject — stick with the questions in the lesson. In each discussion session, the Leader is responsible for finishing **all** of the *Questions for Understanding* and at least two *Questions for Application*.

- <u>Use the Answer Key carefully</u>. It will add insight to the group discussion. Do not present the Answer Key as the standard to which the group is supposed to attain in their written pre-work. The Answer Key is much more detailed than any one participant's answers and brings in information from sources not available to the group. Please do NOT photocopy and hand out the Answer Key as this can set up unrealistic expectations for each participant's contributions.

- All the questions can be answered from the film lessons, the Commentary in the Study Guide, and from the references provided to the Bible passages and the *Catechism*. The small group discussion will be much more fruitful if participants complete the questions in writing before the discussion.

6. **Promote participation by all group members.**

During the first session, develop some ground rules for participation. It's helpful to prepare your group with an understanding of the overall program. Please set expectations at a high level so the participants can truly commit to grow into better disciples and evangelists.

Some suggestions to share with the participants for setting expectations and ground rules for discussion:

- **Pray**: Ask for guidance from the Holy Spirit and keep an open mind.

- **Commit to the study**: Plan to come each time and stay for the whole session. Obviously emergencies come up, but the goal is to begin the study with an attitude of commitment to attend all sessions. Encourage completion of lessons even if someone misses the session.

- **Everyone participates:** The Leader may say something like, "If you tend to talk a lot, please listen more. If you prefer to listen, please pick at least one of your answers to share with the group. Questions are welcome—don't feel you have to have the answer to talk."

- **Be Prepared:** Stress the importance of reading the commentary and writing down answers to the questions; however, tell them to come even if they didn't have time to prepare. They will still benefit from hearing others discuss the lesson and from watching the video. Encourage members to complete their lessons when they are absent so they can keep up with the study. You may want a second set of videos to lend when someone misses a session.

- **Guarantee confidentiality:** All things discussed in the group are to be kept confidential. This is very important, especially for the *Questions for Application* in each lesson.

PROGRAM STRUCTURE OPTIONS

<u>NUMBER OF SESSIONS</u>: **13**

<u>DURATION OF EACH SESSION</u>: **90 minutes**

<u>PROGRAM FLOW</u>:
There are two options for presenting this program in 13 sessions as summarized in the chart below. Option #1 requires individual preparation before viewing the film lesson, while Option #2 requires individual preparation **after** viewing the film lesson. Both options conclude with the discussion group in each lesson.

	STRUCTURE OPTION #1	STRUCTURE OPTION #2
ORIENTATION	- Orientation Activities (see below) - Assign *Francis - Part I* reading/questions	- Orientation Activities (see below) - Show *Francis - Part I* video - Assign *Francis - Part I* reading/questions
2ND SESSION	- Show *Francis - Part I* video - Discuss *Francis - Part I* questions - Assign *Francis - Part II* reading/questions	- Discuss *Francis - Part I* questions - Show *Francis - Part II* - Assign *Francis - Part II* reading/questions
3RD SESSION	- Show *Francis - Part II* video - Discuss *Francis - Part II* questions - Assign *Aquinas - Part I* reading/questions	- Discuss *Francis - Part II* questions - Show *Aquinas - Part I* video - Assign *Aquinas - Part I* reading/questions
4TH SESSION	- Show *Aquinas - Part I* video - Discuss *Aquinas - Part I* questions - Assign *Aquinas - Part II* reading/questions	- Discuss *Aquinas - Part I* questions - Show *Aquinas - Part II* video - Assign *Aquinas - Part II* reading/questions
5TH SESSION	- Show *Aquinas - Part II* video - Discuss *Aquinas - Part II* questions - Assign *Catherine - Part I* reading/questions	- Discuss *Aquinas - Part II* questions - Show *Catherine - Part I* video - Assign *Catherine - Part I* reading/questions
6TH SESSION	- Show *Catherine - Part I* video - Discuss *Catherine - Part I* questions - Assign *Catherine - Part II* reading/questions	- Discuss *Catherine - Part I* questions - Show *Catherine - Part II* video - Assign *Catherine - Part II* reading/questions
7TH - 13TH SESSIONS	CONTINUE AS ABOVE for *Catherine - Part II, Newman, Chesterton,* *and Michelangelo*	CONTINUE AS ABOVE for *Catherine - Part II, Newman, Chesterton,* *and Michelangelo*

FIRST SESSION ORIENTATION ACTIVITIES

Orientation:

- Confirm pre-registered participants
- Register walk-ins
- Distribute Study Guides and nametags to all (**Note:** *order 15-20% more than pre-registrations for unexpected "walk-ins" during the first few sessions*).
- Opening Prayer
- Present overview of Program Structure, explaining the session flow for either Option #1 or Option #2 above.
- Present "Program Expectations" and/or "Ground Rules for Small Group Discussion." The Program Coordinator should present the ground rules and expectations for participation. *Please see suggested list of expectations and ground rules on page 15.*
- Meet in the assigned small discussion groups for introductions. You could use an ice-breaker game, such as:

    "Say three things about yourself that few people know. One should be false and the two others, true. Have the group guess which is false."
    "To what saint are you particularly attracted? Why?"
    "Why did you choose to join this program?"

- Each small Group Leader should discuss the ground rules presented by the Program Coordinator, and adapt or add to them as their group members desire.
- In your small groups, skim through the commentary and questions for *Francis-Part I* in the Study Guide. Explain how to prepare the questions for the next session.

SESSION OVERVIEW

1. **Gathering and Opening** (5 minutes)

Many groups offer refreshments and encourage their participants to come a few minutes early for some time of fellowship. The coordinator should begin the session promptly. It is very important to start and finish on time.

Officially begin each session with an Opening Prayer. Select the prayer found on the included Prayer Cards, or use another prayer (suggestions below). If you have a priest or deacon participating, he can lead the Opening Prayer and offer a few words related to the session topic. Try to avoid another lecture here—the film serves as the "lecture" and teaching part of the program. You can also sing a hymn together to set a reverent tone.

The Prayer to the Holy Spirit (below) is an appropriate prayer to use to begin each session. You can copy this prayer so everyone may pray along:

> *Come Holy Spirit. Fill the hearts of your faithful*
> *And kindle in them the fire of your love.*
> *Send forth your spirit, and they shall be created*
> *And you shall renew the face of the earth.*
>
> *Oh God, who by the light of the Holy Spirit,*
> *Did instruct the hearts of the faithful,*
> *Grant that by the same Holy Spirit*
> *We may be truly wise and ever enjoy His consolations*
> *Through Christ, our Lord. Amen.*

Also, the Prayer to St. Michael the Archangel can be used as an opening or closing prayer:

> *St. Michael the Archangel defend us in battle.*
> *Be our protection against the wickedness and snares of the Devil.*
> *May God rebuke him, we humbly pray,*
> *And do thou, O Prince of the heavenly hosts, by the power of God,*
> *Cast into hell Satan, and all the evil spirits*
> *Who roam through the world*
> *Seeking the destruction of souls. Amen.*

2. **Video Viewing** (25-40 minutes)

- **Structure Option #1:** Video viewed before discussion
- **Structure Option #2:** Video viewed after discussion of prior video's Study Guide questions

    The entire group of participants comes together to watch the video for each session. During the viewing of the video, participants can follow along and take notes using the Outline in the Study Guide at the beginning of each lesson.

3. **Discussion Groups** (60 minutes)

- **Structure Option #1:** Discussion happens during the same session as the companion video is viewed (question prep **before** video viewing)
- **Structure Option #2:** Discussion happens the session after the companion video is viewed (question prep **after** video viewing)

    Break into small groups for discussion of the *Questions for Understanding* and at least two *Questions for Application*. If you find that you do not have time to complete all the *Questions for Application*, it is helpful to let participants know ahead of time which Application questions you will discuss.

    While the Group Discussion Leader should not provide any answers to the *Questions for Understanding*, he or she should share during the *Questions for Application* in order to build trust and fellowship within the small group.

4. **Closing Prayer** (<5 minutes)

    If you did not open with the special prayer found on the Prayer Cards, please use it as a closing prayer to help everyone meditate on the lives of these amazing Catholics.

VIDEO CONTENTS

ONLINE RESOURCES

The following resources can be found online at *pivotalplayers.wordonfire.org/#support*

Advertising

- Poster
- Flyer
- Bulletin Announcement
- Announcement from the Pulpit

Study Program Support

- Registration Form
- Certificate of Completion
- Evaluation of Program Survey
- *Managing Personalities for Effective Group Discussion*

ST. FRANCIS *of* ASSISI
The Reformer

CATHOLICISM
THE PIVOTAL PLAYERS
VOLUME I

St. Francis of Assisi Study Guide written by Fr. Raniero Cantalamessa

✠

ST. FRANCIS *of* ASSISI
The Reformer

STUDY GUIDE WRITTEN BY
Fr. Raniero Cantalamessa

Fr. Raniero Cantalamessa is a Franciscan Capuchin priest, ordained in 1958. In 1980, he was appointed by St. John Paul II as Preacher to the Papal Household and confirmed in that position by Pope Benedict XVI in 2005, and again by Pope Francis in 2013. In this capacity he preaches during Advent and Lent in the presence of the Pope, the cardinals, bishops, and other prelates of the Roman Curia and the general superiors of religious orders.

Cantalamessa holds doctoral degrees in theology and classical literature. He has served as a member of the International Theological Commission and the Catholic Delegation for the dialogue with the Pentecostal Churches.

ST. FRANCIS *of* ASSISI
The Reformer
VIDEO OUTLINE — PART I

I. INTRODUCTION

    A. Man of contradiction: simple and humble, yet a deeply troubling and unnerving figure

    B. Represented back-to-basics evangelization with a return to the radicality of the Gospel

II. EARLY YEARS

    A. Born in 1182 in Assisi, son of Pica and Pietro Bernardone, a cloth merchant

    B. Not a proficient writer; loved to sing, especially songs of French troubadours

    C. Worked in his father's shop and liked fine clothes, money, and partying

    D. Sought fame, joined battles, eventually imprisoned

    E. Had a powerful dream where Christ asked him whom he would serve: the master or the servant

    F. Back in Assisi, the things that used to satisfy him did not anymore

III. CONVERSION

    A. Began to give things away to the poor

    B. Embraced leper and was filled with happiness

    C. Radical detachment from goods of the world and attachment to the purposes of God

IV. REBUILD MY CHURCH

    A. In 1206 at San Damiano, a small church in ruins, Francis heard Christ speak from the Cross, telling him to rebuild his house

    B. Sold cloth from father's shop to fund renovations

    C. Put on trial before bishop and came to renounce father and declare total devotion to God as his only Father

    D. Solely dependent on God's providence; begged for sustenance

    E. Others began to join him, selling possessions to fund his mission

IV. ESTABLISHMENT OF THE ORDER
  A. In 1209, along with twelve disciples, Francis went to see Pope Innocent III to get permission to begin an order
  B. Corruption rampant at the time; initially dismissed by pope
  C. Came back and was given permission after pope remembered a dream about *il Poverello* (little poor man) holding up the Lateran church
  D. Called order the "Friars Minor" as they were to take the lowest place
  E. Vows of poverty, chastity, and obedience

ST. FRANCIS *of* ASSISI

THE CONVERSION
of ST. FRANCIS

To understand something of Francis' adventure, it is necessary to begin with his conversion. Sources record different descriptions of this event, with notable variations among them. Fortunately we have an absolutely reliable source, which dispenses us from selecting among the different versions. We have the testimony of Francis himself in his testament, his own *ipsissima verba* ("the very words," as is said of Christ's words reliably reported in the Gospel):

> The Lord gave me, Brother Francis, thus to begin doing penance: for when I was in sin, it seemed too bitter for me to see lepers. And the Lord himself led me among them and I showed mercy to them. And when I left them, what had seemed bitter to me was turned into sweetness of soul and body. And afterwards I delayed a little and left the world.[1]

Historians rightly insist on the fact that in the beginning Francis did not choose poverty, and even less so pauperism; he chose the poor! The change was motivated more by the commandment, "Love thy neighbor as thyself," than by the counsel, "If you wish to be perfect, go, sell all that you have and give it to the poor, then come and follow me." It was compassion for poor people, more than the search for his own perfection, that moved him—charity more than poverty.

All this is true, but it still does not touch the core of Francis' conversion. His focus on the poor was the effect of the change, not its cause. The true choice was much more radical. It was not about choosing between wealth and poverty, nor between the rich and the poor, nor between belonging to one class rather than another. It was about choosing between himself and God, between saving his life or losing it for the Gospel.

There have been some who came to Christ out of love for the poor (for instance, in times closer to us, Simone Weil). There have been others who came to the poor out of love for Christ. Francis belongs to the latter group. The profound motive for his conversion was not social in nature but evangelical. Jesus had formulated the law once and for all in one of the most solemn and most authentic phrases of the Gospel:

> If anyone wishes to come after me, he must deny himself, take up his cross and follow me. For whoever wishes to save his life will lose it; but whoever loses his life for my sake will find it. (Matt 16:24-25)

When Francis did the unthinkable and kissed a leper out of mercy, he denied himself in what was most "bitter" and repugnant to his nature. Francis did not go to the lepers spontaneously, by his own will, or because he was moved by human and religious compassion. "The Lord," he writes, "led me among them." It is this small detail that is the origin of everything.

✝

HOW ST. FRANCIS REFORMED THE CHURCH

How was it that such an interior and personal event as the conversion of the young Francis launched a movement that changed the face of the Church of his time and has had such a powerful effect in history up until our own day?

We must look at the situation during that period. In Francis' time, more or less everyone acknowledged the need for reform in the Church. Tensions and deep lacerations scarred the body of the Church. On one side was the institutional Church—the pope, the bishops, the higher clergy—worn out by perennial conflicts and by their very close alliance with the empire. It was a Church seen as distant, involved in matters far beyond the interests of the people. With them were the great religious orders, among them the Cistercians,

4

many of which flourished in culture and spirituality, thanks to the reforms of the eleventh century. However, many orders were identified with the great landowners, the feudal lords of the time, who were remote from the problems and the tenor of life of the common people.

On the opposite side, there was a society that was beginning to emigrate from the countryside to the city in search of greater freedom from different forms of servitude. This part of society identified the Church with the dominant classes from which they felt the need to free themselves. Because of this, they would gladly take sides with those who contradicted the Church and fought against her—heretics, radical movements, and groups, that preached poverty—while they sympathized with the lower clergy, who were often spiritually not at the level of the prelates but closer to the people.

There were, therefore, strong tensions that everyone sought to exploit to their own advantage. The hierarchy sought to respond to these tensions by improving its organization and suppressing abuses, both within its leadership (e.g., simony, concubinage of priests) and outside of it (i.e., in society). The hostile groups sought instead to bring the tensions to a head, radicalizing the conflict with the hierarchy and giving rise to movements that were more or less schismatic. All of them used the ideal of evangelical poverty and simplicity against the Church, turning it into a hostile weapon and making it something other than a spiritual ideal to be lived in humility.

We are accustomed to seeing Francis as the man sent by Providence, who picks up these popular calls for renewal, defuses the voltage of controversy, and brings many back into the Church. In this view, Francis is a sort of mediator between the rebellious heretics and the institutional Church. This is how his mission is presented in a well-known manual of Church history:

> Given that the wealth and power of the Church was often seen as a source of grave evils, and provided the heretics of the time with arguments for the main accusations against her, in some pious souls the noble desire was awakened to revive the poor life of Christ and of the primitive Church, and thus be able to influence the people more effectively by word and example.[2]

One must be careful not to draw the wrong conclusions from the famous words of the Crucifix of San Damiano: "Francis, go and repair my Church, which as you see, is in ruins."[3] The sources themselves assure us that he understood those words in the rather modest sense of repairing the little church of San Damiano materially.

It was his disciples and biographers who interpreted those words—and rightly so, it must be said—as referring to the institutional Church, not just to the church building. He always kept to his literal interpretation, and, in fact, continued to repair other small, ruined churches on the outskirts of Assisi.

Even the dream of Innocent III, in which he is said to have seen the *Poverello* supporting the collapsing Church of St. John Lateran on his shoulders, does not tell us anything more. Supposing that the event is historical (a similar event is also related about Saint Dominic), the dream was the pope's, not Francis'! He never saw himself as we see him today in Giotto's frescoes. This is what it means to be a reformer by way of holiness: being so without knowing it.

If he did not wish to be a reformer, what then did Francis want to be and do? Here, too, we are fortunate enough to have the saint's direct testimony in his testament:

> And after the Lord gave me some brothers, no one showed me what I had to do; but the Most High Himself revealed to me that I should live according to the pattern of the Holy Gospel. And I had this written down simply and in a few words and the Lord Pope confirmed it for me.[4]

He alludes to the moment when, during Mass, he heard the passage of the Gospel where Jesus sends his disciples: "He sent them out to preach the Kingdom of God and to heal the sick. And he said to them, 'Take nothing for your journey, no staff, no bag, nor bread, nor money; and do not have two tunics'" (Luke 9:2-3).[5]

It was a dazzling revelation, the kind that gives direction to the whole of life. From that day onwards his mission was clear: a simple and radical return to the real Gospel lived and preached by Jesus, by restoring in the world the way and style of the life of Jesus and of the Apostles. Writing the Rule for his friars, he began thus: "The Rule and life of the friars is this, namely, to observe the holy Gospel of our Lord Jesus Christ."

Francis did not build a theory on his discovery or turn it into a program for the reform of the Church. He accomplished the reform in himself, thus tacitly pointing out to the Church the only way out of the crisis: to come close to the Gospel again and to come close to the people again, in particular to the humble and the poor.

Francis did in his day what was intended at the time of Vatican II: pull down the bastions; put an end to the isolation of the Church and bring her back into contact with the people. One of the factors that obscured the Gospel was the shift from a service-based authority to one focused on power, which produced endless conflicts inside and outside the Church. Francis, for his part, resolved the problem evangelically. In his Order—and this was totally new—the superiors would be called ministers, meaning servants, and all the others friars, meaning brothers.

PRAYER *of* ST. FRANCIS

Lord, make me an instrument of your peace.
Where there is hatred, let me sow love;
where there is injury, pardon;
where there is doubt, faith;
where there is despair, hope;
where there is darkness, light;
where there is sadness, joy.

O, Divine Master, grant that I may not so much seek to be
consoled as to console;
to be understood as to understand;
to be loved as to love;

For it is in giving that we receive;
it is in pardoning that we are pardoned;
it is in dying that we are born again to eternal life.

ST. FRANCIS *of* ASSISI: *The Reformer*

QUESTIONS FOR UNDERSTANDING

1. What moved Francis to embrace the leper, which was an act most repugnant to his nature? (Matt 16:24-25; 2 Cor 5:15-20; Rom 14:7-8; Gal 2:20)

2. After his conversion, Francis dedicated himself to the corporal and spiritual works of mercy. What are those? Why are they important? (CCC 2447; Matt 25:31-46; James 2:14-17; 1 John 3:11, 16-18)

3. How was the lifestyle of St. Francis and his Friars Minor similar to the lifestyle of the early Christian community? (Acts 2:42-47, 32-35; Luke 9:1-3)

- Community
- Francis gave up himself
- Do we sacrificin' & givin - up
- Sacrifcin'in different ways

4. Where did Francis' joy come from? How did it affect his evangelism? (1 Pet 1:8-9; Rom 15:13; CCC 736, 1832, 1829)

QUESTIONS FOR APPLICATION

1. After his conversion, the material world did not satisfy Francis as it had before. Describe a time when you sought out something of this world (e.g., wealth, pleasure, power, honor), but when you obtained it, you were not as satisfied as you expected. How did you grow in spiritual wisdom through that experience?

2. Slowly pray the Prayer of St. Francis (found on page 7) and spend 5-10 minutes meditating on it and on its author. What comes to mind in terms of your own life?

3. Who are the "lepers" in your life? How do you serve them? What additional step can you take this week to love them more?

EXCERPT FROM POPE FRANCIS' ENCYCLICAL *Laudato Si'*

"Laudato si', mi' Signore"—"Praise be to you, my Lord." In the words of this beautiful canticle, Saint Francis of Assisi reminds us that our common home is like a sister with whom we share our life and a beautiful mother who opens her arms to embrace us. "Praise be to you, my Lord, through our Sister, Mother Earth, who sustains and governs us, and who produces various fruit with colored flowers and herbs."

I do not want to write this Encyclical without turning to that attractive and compelling figure, whose name I took as my guide and inspiration when I was elected Bishop of Rome. I believe that Saint Francis is the example par excellence of care for the vulnerable and of an integral ecology lived out joyfully and authentically. He is the patron saint of all who study and work in the area of ecology, and he is also much loved by non-Christians. He was particularly concerned for God's creation and for the poor and outcast. He loved, and was deeply loved for his joy, his generous self-giving, his openheartedness. He was a mystic and a pilgrim who lived in simplicity and in wonderful harmony with God, with others, with nature, and with himself. He shows us just how inseparable the bond is between concern for nature, justice for the poor, commitment to society, and interior peace.

Francis helps us to see that an integral ecology calls for openness to categories which transcend the language of mathematics and biology, and take us to the heart of what it is to be human. Just as happens when we fall in love with someone, whenever he would gaze at the sun, the moon, or the smallest of animals, he burst into song, drawing all other creatures into his praise. He communed with all creation, even preaching to the flowers, inviting them "to praise the Lord, just as if they were endowed with reason."

His response to the world around him was so much more than intellectual appreciation or economic calculus, for to him each and every creature was a sister united to him by bonds of affection. That is why he felt called to care for all that exists. His disciple Saint Bonaventure tells us that "from a reflection on the primary source of all things, filled with even more abundant piety, he would call creatures, no matter how small, by the name of 'brother' or 'sister.'"

Such a conviction cannot be written off as naive romanticism, for it affects the choices which determine our behavior. If we approach nature and the environment without this openness to awe and wonder, if we no longer speak the language of fraternity and beauty in our relationship with the world, our attitude will be that of masters, consumers, ruthless exploiters, unable to set limits on their immediate needs. By contrast, if we feel intimately united with all that exists, then sobriety and care will well up spontaneously. The poverty and austerity of Saint Francis were no mere veneer of asceticism, but something much more radical: a refusal to turn reality into an object simply to be used and controlled.

What is more, Saint Francis, faithful to Scripture, invites us to see nature as a magnificent book in which God speaks to us and grants us a glimpse of his infinite beauty and goodness. "Through the greatness and the beauty of creatures one comes to know by analogy their maker" (Wis 13:5); indeed, "his eternal power and divinity have been made known through his works since the creation of the world" (Rom 1:20). For this reason, Francis asked that part of the friary garden always be left untouched, so that wild flowers and herbs could grow there, and those who saw them could raise their minds to God, the Creator of such beauty. Rather than a problem to be solved, the world is a joyful mystery to be contemplated with gladness and praise.

ST. FRANCIS *of* ASSISI
The Reformer
VIDEO OUTLINE — PART II

I. GROWTH OF THE ORDER

    A. Many men joined the Friars Minor

    B. St. Clare founded female Franciscan order: Poor Ladies

    C. Francis had a special connection to animals

        1. Preached to birds

        2. Tamed the wolf of Gubbio

    D. Missions near and far

        1. Sent brothers to Christian lands and they did not fare well, except in England

        2. Sent brothers to non-Christian lands and some were executed

        3. Joined crusades and interacted with the Muslim Sultan himself

    E. Experienced perfect joy in suffering for Christ

II. STIGMATA AND DEATH

    A. Went on spiritual retreat in La Verna, Italy, in 1224

    B. Asked for two graces: feel full pain of Christ's Passion, and love Christ with the love that made him sacrifice himself for us

    C. Received stigmata

    D. Back to Assisi; suffering from eye disease and effects of stigmata

    E. Died singing and in total submission to God

III. WHY A PIVOTAL PLAYER?

    A. Francis' life showed that one can realize the Christian ideal by living according to the Gospel *literally*

    B. This lifestyle unleashes enormous, transformative power in the world

ST. FRANCIS *of* ASSISI

ST. FRANCIS *and* *the* INCARNATE WORD

Three years before his death, St. Francis initiated the Christmas tradition of the crib, or "crèche," known today as the Nativity scene. Thomas of Celano, a thirteenth-century friar and biographer, records its origin:

> Around fifteen days prior to the birthday of the Lord, Francis said, "If you wish to celebrate the approaching feast of the Lord in Greccio, hurry and carefully prepare the things I tell you. For I wish to enact the memory of that babe who was born in Bethlehem, to see as much as is possible with my own body the discomfort of his infant needs, how he lay in the manger, and how with an ox and an ass standing by, he rested on hay..."
>
> The manger is prepared, hay is carried in, and the ox and ass are led to the spot. There simplicity is given a place of honor, poverty is exalted, humility is commended and out of Greccio a new Bethlehem is made.

The importance of Francis' crèche lies not so much in the fact itself or in the spectacular consequences it has had in the Christian tradition, but in the novelty of the saint's understanding of the mystery of the Incarnation.

Francis restored "flesh and blood" to the mysteries of Christianity, which were often "disincarnate" and reduced to concepts in theological schools and books. At least one scholar credits Francis with creating the conditions necessary for the birth of modern Renaissance art, in as much as it frees sacred persons and events from the stylized rigidity of the past and confers on them concreteness and life.[6]

For Francis of Assisi, Christmas was the feast that had the power to release all the capacity for joy that was in his heart, which was immense. At Christmas, he literally did foolish things.

> He wanted the poor and hungry to be filled by the rich, and oxen and asses to be spoiled with extra feed and hay. "If ever I speak with the Emperor," he would say, "I will beg him to issue a general decree that all who can should throw wheat and grain along the roads, so that on the day of such a great solemnity the birds may have an abundance, especially our sisters the larks."[7]

He would become like one of those children whose eyes are full of wonder before the crib. His biographer tells us that during the Christmas service at Greccio, whenever he spoke the name "Bethlehem" he would fill his mouth with sound, and even more with tender affection, producing a sound similar to a bleating sheep. And every time he said "Babe of Bethlehem" or "Jesus," he would lick his lips, as if to relish and retain all the sweetness of those words.[8]

But for Francis, the humility of the Incarnation didn't end in the crib. Christ continues to descend into the lowest and darkest areas of life. Certain Fathers of the Church have said that due to the Incarnation, the Word has, in a certain sense, assumed every man because of the *way* in which the Incarnation happened. The Word assumed the poor, the humble, and the suffering by identifying himself with them.

St. Francis was so conscious of this that one day he said to a companion who had misjudged a poor man:

> Whenever you see a poor person you ought to consider Him in whose name he comes, that is, Christ, who came to take on our poverty and weakness. This man's poverty and weakness is a mirror for us in which we should see and consider lovingly the poverty and weakness of our Lord Jesus Christ, which He endured in His body for the salvation of the human race.[9]

In the poor, there is certainly not the same kind of presence of Christ that there is in the Eucharist and in the other sacraments, but it is a presence that is still very true and very real. Jesus "instituted" this sign as he instituted the Eucharist. He who pronounced over the bread the words, "This is my Body," said these same words also referring to the poor. When speaking of what had been done or not done for the hungry, the thirsty, the prisoners, the naked, and the exiled, he solemnly declared, "You did it to me" and "You did not do it to me." This, in fact, is the same as saying, "I was that wounded person in need of some bread, that old man who was dying with cold on the sidewalk!" "The Council Fathers," wrote Jean Guitton, a lay observer at Vatican II, "rediscovered the sacrament of poverty, the presence of Christ under the species of those who suffer."[10]

The poor person is also a "vicar of Christ," one who takes the place of Christ in the passive, not active, sense. In other words, not in the sense that what the poor person does is as if Christ did it, but in the sense that what is done to the poor person is as if it were done to Christ. It is true, as St. Leo the Great wrote, that after the Ascension, "all that was visible in our Lord Jesus Christ has passed into the sacramental signs of the Church."[11] It is equally true that, from the existential point of view, it has also passed into the poor and into all those of whom he said, "you did it to me."

THE STIGMATA

"Stigmata" is the plural form of the Greek word that means a mark or brand (i.e., to identify an animal or slave), and is used to refer to marks or wounds of Christ's crucifixion that have appeared on men and women since the thirteenth century. Some scholars suspect that St. Paul himself may have been the first to have the stigmata, for he said: "I bear the marks of Jesus on my body" (Gal 6:17).

The first recorded stigmatic in history was St. Francis of Assisi. His original biographer, Thomas of Celano, described Francis' wounds in his 1230 book, *First Life of St. Francis*:

His wrists and feet seemed to be pierced by nails, with the heads of the nails appearing on his wrists and on the upper sides of his feet, the points appearing on the other side. The marks were round on the palm of each hand but elongated on the other side, and small pieces of flesh jutting out from the rest took on the appearance of the nail-ends, bent and driven back. In the same way the marks of nails were impressed on his feet and projected beyond the rest of the flesh. Moreover, his right side had a large wound as if it had been pierced with a spear, and it often bled so that his tunic and trousers were soaked with his sacred blood.

Not all stigmatics exhibit the same wounds. Some have nail wounds on their hands, wrists, and feet, and others also carry a wound in the side where Jesus was pierced with a sword. Some show wounds on their foreheads, reminiscent of those from the crown of thorns. Others cry or sweat blood or have wounds on the back, as from scourging. In some cases, the blood from the wounds is said to have a pleasing, perfumed aroma, often called the *odor of sanctity*.

Some stigmatics, such as St. Catherine of Siena, feel the pain of wounds with no external marks, and so have an "invisible stigmata."

†

HOW TO IMITATE ST. FRANCIS TODAY

What does Francis' experience say to us today? What can we—all of us, right now—imitate in his life? Be it those whom God calls to reform the Church by the way of holiness, or those who feel called to renew her by way of criticism, or those he himself calls to reform her through the office they hold? We can imitate the thing that started Francis' spiritual adventure: his conversion from ego to God, his denial of self. This is how true reformers are born. Those who really change something in the Church are people who seriously *decide* to die to themselves. It is an enterprise that lasts a lifetime and beyond if, as St. Teresa of Avila jokingly said, our self-love dies twenty minutes after we do.

Silvanus of Mount Athos, a holy Orthodox monk, said: "To be truly free, one must begin to bind oneself." Men such as these are free with the freedom of the Spirit; nothing stops them and nothing frightens them anymore. They become reformers by way of holiness, and not only by way of office.

But what does Jesus mean by proposing that one deny oneself? Is such a proposal still valid in a world that speaks only of self-realization and self-affirmation? Denial is never an end in itself or an ideal in itself. The most important thing is the positive part; it is to follow Christ, to possess Christ. To say "no" to oneself is the means; to say "yes" to Christ is the end. Paul represents self-denial as a sort of law of the spirit: "If with the help of the Spirit you put to death the deeds of the body you will live" (Rom 8:13). This, as we see, is a dying in order to live; the very opposite of the philosophical view of human life as "a living to die" (Heidegger).

It is all about choosing the foundation on which we want to build our lives: on our ego or on Christ? In Paul's language, do we want to live "for ourselves" or "for the Lord"? (cf. 2 Cor 5:15; Rom 14:7-8). To live "for ourselves" means to live for our own comfort, our own glory, and our own advancement. To live "for the Lord" means that we intentionally put Christ's glory and the interests of the Kingdom and the Church first. Every "no" said to oneself out of love, small or big as it may be, is a "yes" said to Christ.

We must not delude ourselves. It is not a matter of knowing everything about Christian denial or about how beautiful and necessary it is. The point is, we must do something about it and put it into practice. A great ancient spiritual teacher said:

In a short time one may cut off ten of one's own desires, and I will tell you how. Let us suppose that someone is walking a short distance; he sees something and the thought says to him, "Look over there." He replies to the thought, "I will not look," and he cuts off his desire and does not look. Or he meets some others who are talking idly among themselves and the thought says to him, "You say a word also," but he cuts off his desire and does not speak.

This ancient father gives examples drawn from the monastic life. But they can be easily updated and adapted to the life of everyone. Let's say you meet, perhaps not a leper like Francis, but a poor man whom you know will ask you for something. Your old nature pushes you to cross to the other side of the street, but instead, you do violence to yourself and go to meet him, perhaps giving him only a greeting or a smile, if you cannot do more. Or you are given an opportunity to profit from something illegally and you say no, thereby denying yourself. When you are contradicted in one of your ideas and wounded in your pride, you want to fight back strongly, but you become silent and wait—you have broken your ego. You believe you have been wronged, treated unjustly, and not given the job you deserve. You want everyone to know about it, to shut yourself off in a silent rebuke. But you say "no," break the silence, smile, and reopen the dialogue. You have denied yourself and saved charity. The opportunities are endless.

One sign of progress in the struggle against our ego is the capacity, or at least the effort, to rejoice at the good done or the promotion received by another, as if it were our own. "Blessed is that servant," writes Francis in one of his admonitions, "who no more exalts himself over the good the Lord says or does through him than over what He says or does through another."

A difficult goal, but Francis' experience has shown us what can come from the denial of self in response to grace. The prize is the joy of being able to say with Paul and with Francis: "It is no longer I who live, but Christ lives in me" (Gal 2:19). And it will mean the beginning of joy and peace here on earth. With his "perfect joy," Francis is a true witness to "the joy of the Gospel," the Evangelii gaudium.

ST. FRANCIS *and* ST. CLARE

St. Francis inspired many to join his "Friars Minor;" however, one follower took this inspiration in a whole new direction by founding a convent called the "Order of Poor Ladies."

Lady Clare Sciffi was born into nobility about 12 years after Francis' birth. The families were connected and both lived in Assisi, although Francis came from a successful, but not noble, merchant's family. His father and his mother encouraged him to develop a relationship with the Sciffi family. His father desired that his son mix with nobility and eventually become a knight. His mother was interested in the Sciffi family more out of charity, as she had sent Francis to their castle with a healing remedy for Clare when she was 3 and ill with a fever.

When Lady Clare turned 18, her father informed her that a knight from Perugia was coming for her hand in marriage in a few short weeks. Having known Francis all her life, and having heard him preach the gospel of poverty, she asked him to shelter her so she could devote her life to Christ. One night, under the cover of darkness, she fled from her castle with her cousin, Pacifica, and was met by the Friars Minor carrying torches to light her way.

Francis cut Clare and Pacifica's hair, gave them veils, and took them to a nearby convent for safekeeping. A few days later, Clare's younger sister Agnes also ran away to join the convent. Clare's father was furious and tried to bring his two daughters home, but to no avail. As they clung to the altar, the girls told him they had now pledged their lives to God and to the poor.

Clare's order grew, with other noble ladies renouncing their wealth, and she became the first woman to write a rule of religious life for women. After her father's death, even her mother, other sister, and aunt joined the convent. San Damiano, the small church that Francis had restored after hearing Jesus' voice from the Cross, was transformed into a convent for the new order. The "Order of Poor Ladies" dedicated themselves to growing food for the poor and tending the sick.

Sister Clare lived for many years after Francis' death, and continued to carry on the Franciscan mission. One famous story of her sanctity comes from wartime Italy. The invading Muslim army encountered the convent on their way to Assisi and began to climb its walls, planning to kill all they found. Clare rushed from the chapel where she was praying, leaned out the window, and held high the Blessed Sacrament. The attackers were struck by a blinding light and retreated, refusing to continue the march into Assisi. Through her prayers and courage, all the nuns and the people of Assisi were saved. She died in 1253 and was named a saint two years later.

QUESTIONS FOR UNDERSTANDING

1. How did Francis "restore the 'flesh and blood' to the mysteries of Christianity"? Why was this particularly important at this time in Church history?

2. In the video, Bishop Barron talks about two graces that Francis prayed for about a year before he died. What did he pray for and how did God answer his prayer?

3. Francis embraced suffering with great joy, even seeming to seek it out. Why do you think he did that? How is suffering related to penance? (Rom 8:16-17; Col 1:24; CCC 977, 1494, 1434-35, 1032)

4. In what way would you describe St. Francis as a "reformer" during his lifetime? How do you believe the reform took shape after his death from the seeds he had planted? (CCC 1430-32, Ps 51:12; Rom 12:2)

QUESTIONS FOR APPLICATION

1. What can you do to "radically" change your habits to better follow the Gospel? If this question is difficult for you to answer, spend some time in prayer and then read the Sermon on the Mount (Matt 5-7). Reflect on what meaning there might be for you in these verses.

2. How has your view of suffering changed since learning about St. Francis? What can you do to incorporate these changes in the future?

3. What internal "reform" do you need in your heart in order to be fully abandoned to God as Francis was?

ENDNOTES

✝ PART I

1) Francis of Assisi, *Early Documents, Vol. I* (New York: New City Press, 1999), 124 (hereafter quoted as ED plus volume number).

2) K. Bihlmeyer – H. Tuchle, *Storia della Chiesa*, II (Brescia, 2009), 239.

3) Celano, *Vita Secunda*, VI,10 (ED, II), 249.

4) *The Testament*, 14.15 (ED, I), 125.

5) *The Legend of the Three Companions*, VIII (ED,II), 8.

✝ PART II

6) H. Thode, *Franz of Assisi und die Anfänge der Kunst des Renaissance in Italien*, Berlin 1885.

7) Celano, *Vita Secunda*, 151 (ED, II), 375.

8) Celano, *Vita Prima*, 30 (ED,I), 256.

9) *Legenda Perusina*, 89 (ED, II), 221.

10) J. Guitton, quoted by R. Gil, *Presence of the Poor in the Council, in "Proyección"* 48, 1966, 30.

11) St. Leo the Great, *Discourse 2 on the Ascension*, 2 (PL 54), 398.

12) Dorotheus of Gaza, *Spiritual Works*, I, 20 (SCh 92), 177.

13) *Admonitions XVII* (ED, I, p. 134).

St. Francis'
CANTICLE *of the* SUN

Most high, all powerful, all good Lord! All praise is yours, all glory, all honor, and all blessing. To you, alone, Most High, do they belong. No mortal lips are worthy to pronounce your name.

Be praised, my Lord, through all your creatures, especially through my lord Brother Sun, who brings the day; and you give light through him. And he is beautiful and radiant in all his splendor! Of you, Most High, he bears the likeness.

Be praised, my Lord, through Sister Moon and the stars; in the heavens you have made them, precious and beautiful.

Be praised, my Lord, through Brothers Wind and Air, and clouds and storms, and all the weather, through which you give your creatures sustenance.

Be praised, my Lord, through Sister Water; she is very useful, and humble, and precious, and pure.

Be praised, my Lord, through Brother Fire, through whom you brighten the night. He is beautiful and cheerful, and powerful and strong.

Be praised, my Lord, through our sister Mother Earth, who feeds us and rules us, and produces various fruits with colored flowers and herbs.

Be praised, my Lord, through those who forgive for love of you; through those who endure sickness and trial. Happy those who endure in peace, for by you, Most High, they will be crowned.

Be praised, my Lord, through our Sister Bodily Death, from whose embrace no living person can escape. Woe to those who die in mortal sin! Happy those she finds doing your most holy will. The second death can do no harm to them.

Praise and bless my Lord, and give thanks, and serve him with great humility.

NOTES:

ST. THOMAS AQUINAS

The Theologian

CATHOLICISM

THE PIVOTAL PLAYERS

VOLUME I

St. Thomas Aquinas Study Guide written by Dr. Matthew Levering

ST. THOMAS AQUINAS
The Theologian

STUDY GUIDE WRITTEN BY
Dr. Matthew Levering

Dr. Matthew Levering, one of today's most respected Catholic theologians, holds the Perry Family Foundation Chair of Theology at Mundelein Seminary. He previously taught at the University of Dayton and Ave Maria University. Levering earned a B.A. from the University of North Carolina, an M.T.S. from Duke Divinity School, and a Ph.D. from Boston College.

Levering is a recognized expert on the theology of Thomas Aquinas and has written several books on Aquinas' thought and legacy. He has also written scholarly books on Biblical exegesis, natural law, proofs for God, and the interplay of the Jewish and Christian traditions.

ST. THOMAS AQUINAS
The Theologian
VIDEO OUTLINE — PART I

I.   INTRODUCTION
   A. Huge contributor to the Church and to Western culture
   B. Many roles: philosopher, theologian, scientist, mystic, biblical interpreter, and, most importantly, saint

II. LIFE AND TIMES
   A. Born in Italy in 1225
   B. Sent to Benedictine monastery at age 5 and was there for nine years
      1. Asked a key question at a very young age: "What is God?"
      2. Spent his whole life answering this question
   C. At age 15, went to the University of Naples
      1. Double radical
         a. Devotee of Aristotle
         b. Took vows as a Dominican (mendicant lifestyle) over objections of his family
   D. With Dominican companions, went to Paris and studied under Albert the Great
   E. Accompanied Albert to Cologne as his apprentice and was ordained there
   F. Returned to Paris in 1252 to complete his doctoral studies; in 1256 became a master of theology
      1. Preached on scripture and conducted "disputed questions" forum
   G. "Disputed questions" became the foundation of his seminal work, the *Summa theologiae*, written from 1265–1274
   H. Productive life: over 25 years, 50 volumes of collected works
   I. In 1273, on the Feast of St. Nicholas, something happened and he stopped writing, saying that his writings were "nothing but straw compared to what has been revealed to me."
      1. Took to his bed
      2. Died on the way to the Council of Lyons in 1274

III.   DOCTRINE OF GOD
   A. Thomas' answer to his own question: "What is God?"
   B. God is not a being, but being itself: *ipsum esse subsistens*, the sheer act of "to be" itself
   C. God's essence and existence is one and the same
        1. He is being itself, which has always existed
        2. Man's essence and existence are different (by contrast)
   D. Attributes: eternal, immutable (unchangeable), immaterial, infinite
   E. A personal God who knows and loves himself and overflows with "effervescent love" to create the universe

THE LIFE & TEACHING *of*
ST. THOMAS AQUINAS

Thomas Aquinas was a Dominican friar, a priest, a scholar, a theologian, and a saint. The earliest biographies of Thomas show us a man of prayer who avidly sought personal contact with the living God. He prayed, worshiped, and celebrated the Eucharist as a Dominican friar and priest. He was also a servant of the Church. Commissioned by the pope, he composed liturgical texts for the feast of Corpus Christi; we still sing his eucharistic hymns. He compiled for the pope a "Golden Chain" of the Church Fathers' commentaries on the four Gospels. In an effort to deepen the unity of the Church and to heal the schism between East and West, he responded to texts of Greek theologians on the Trinity. As a member of the Order of Preachers, he preached eloquently and with great erudition, and we still have a number of his sermons, which were delivered largely to students and faculty at the University of Paris and other universities.

Thomas was also an enthusiastic interpreter of Scripture. He was deeply familiar with the ways Scripture reasons, and with the realities about which Scripture speaks. In his theological works, he quoted biblical texts profusely. For example, in the second part alone of his *Summa theologiae*, Aquinas amazingly cites over half of the chapters of the Old Testament, in addition to his numerous quotations of New Testament books. His scriptural commentaries include line-by-line works on all the letters of Paul, the Gospels of Matthew and John, Jeremiah and Isaiah, Job and Lamentations, and some of the Psalms. In these commentaries, he draws upon the earlier commentaries of the Fathers and adds his own insight into the flow of the biblical texts, often interpreting Scripture by means of Scripture.

Thomas was a man of political and ethical insight. He wrote commentaries on Aristotle's *Politics* and *Nicomachean Ethics*, and reflected deeply upon the nature of government, law, and justice, not least in pondering the wisdom of the Mosaic Law. He was also a philosopher in the highest sense, namely, someone who aspires to learn the highest causes of things. In studying the causes of physical things and the divine source of all things, Aquinas wrote lengthy commentaries on Aristotle's *Physics* and *Metaphysics*, Dionysius the Areopagite's *Divine Names*, and the neo-Platonic work *Book of Causes*.

Thomas was not only a philosopher and theologian, but also a mystic. He wrote about the contemplative life, spiritual ecstasy, and rapture. According to his friends and biographers, his life included powerful mystical experiences in which he expressed a complete desire for union with God. At the end of his life, he described his writings as "straw" in comparison with what he had seen in a spiritual vision.

✝

LIFE AND TIMES

A member of a family of minor Italian nobility, Thomas was born in 1224 or 1225 during a period of intense strife. His father and some of his brothers fought in the conflict between Frederick II and the papacy. Another brother became a medieval romantic bard. Thomas was educated by the Benedictines at the very place where Saint Benedict first retreated to contemplate God, Monte Cassino. From Monte Cassino, Thomas went as a teenager to the new University of Naples, one of the first "secular" universities, founded by Frederick II rather than by the Church. Here Thomas encountered the writings of Aristotle, which had found favor in Frederick's court and university. During the period of Thomas' youth, Aristotle's writings were being rediscovered in the West and new translations were being produced. Some Churchmen feared that this would lead to a return of the theological "rationalism" that had been a problem in the 12th century. The great monk-theologians of that century were bold mystics and brilliant scholars, most notably St. Bernard of Clairvaux. But the monks were also worried about the increasing professionalization of theology,

4

which they feared would increase the danger of a dry and rationalistic theology.

In this same 12th century, the Parisian theologian Peter Lombard assisted in the completion of a "gloss", or running commentary, on the whole of Scripture. He also wrote a systematic exposition of the Christian faith, the *Sentences*, which was published in four books and draws heavily upon the writings of Augustine.

The early 13th century saw the rise of the Franciscan and Dominican orders. Both were founded to bring the Gospel beyond the walls of monasteries and to manifest a lifestyle committed to the poverty of Christ and his apostles. These two orders attracted the greatest theological minds of the day, including Albert the Great and Thomas. While a young university student in Naples, Thomas took vows as a Dominican. He did so to his family's shock and dismay; his mother especially tried to turn him from this decision. In 1244, as Thomas journeyed with four other friars to Paris, his mother arranged for him to be waylaid by his brothers who were serving in Frederick's army. His brothers locked him up in the family castle and sought to tempt him away from his vows by sending a naked prostitute into his room. Thomas did not waver during this year in seclusion in his family's home; it is believed that he memorized the whole of Scripture and read Lombard's *Sentences*. When his family finally relented in 1246, Thomas traveled to Paris to study under Albert the Great, who had become a master of theology only a year earlier, but was a seasoned scholar in his early forties. In 1248, Albert was sent to Cologne to preside over the new Dominican house of studies, and Thomas went with him.

Reflecting his varied interests, Thomas' first published works were his brief metaphysical masterpiece, *On Being and Essence*; his commentary on Isaiah, and his massive commentary on the *Sentences of Peter Lombard*. In 1256, Thomas received one of the two Dominican chairs at the University of Paris. He defended mendicant orders (those dependent largely on charitable donations) against criticism mounted by William of St. Amour. To do this, Thomas joined arms with the brilliant young Franciscan contemporary, Bonaventure, who would go on to become Master General of the Franciscan Order and a saint of the Church. As a "teacher of the sacred page," Thomas' primary responsibility was to lecture on Scripture.

His commentaries on Scripture come from these lectures, which were copied down by scribes. In the afternoons, Thomas would often lead discussions of *quaetiones disputatae*, or disputed questions. He and/or his students would debate central theological questions, mustering many oppositions and replies on both sides of the question, and providing a solution. We have a number of Thomas' own disputations, in which he reflects at length and with careful attention to opposed positions on crucial topics. His first published commentary of disputed questions from the late 1250s is, characteristically, on truth.

In the 1260s, when Albert was serving as bishop of Regensburg, Thomas published his *Summa contra Gentiles*, a massive work in which he considers first the realities of faith that can be known by reason, and then those that are known to us only by revelation. He also published lengthy disputed questions on charity, on the power of God, and on evil (including discussions of original sin and on the main vices). Toward the end of the 1260s, he began work on a new introduction to the entirety of theology, with the goal of supplanting Lombard's *Sentences*. This work, the *Summa theologiae*, is widely understood to be his masterpiece. When he stopped writing on December 6, 1273, he had completed most of it, yet it was still incomplete at his death in 1274. In the *Summa theologiae*, one learns how to be a theologian by learning not only the rhythms of biblical and patristic theology—cited so frequently in the *Summa*—but also by learning how to formulate a theological question and how to develop a balanced answer in light of objections that are often strikingly modern.

†

THOMAS' DOCTRINE *of* GOD

Thomas' section on God in the *Summa theologiae* approaches God by the paths that God has given us. For Thomas, it is significant that before revealing himself in Jesus Christ as Father, Son, and Holy Spirit, God reveals himself to Moses as "I am." Recall that in Exodus 3:14, God speaks to Moses out of the burning bush—a symbol of energy that does not deplete itself—and tells Moses that he is the "God of Abraham, Isaac, and Jacob" and that his name is "I am" or "I am who am." In Hebrew, this name could also be "I am who I am" or "I will be who I will be"; but those that translated Exodus from Hebrew into Greek, in the ancient *Septuagint*, translated the name as "I am who am." The main point for Thomas is that God is sheer being; only God can identify himself simply by using the verb "to be." As absolute, unrestricted being, God is able to be precisely what Genesis 1-2 tells us God is: the Creator of all finite beings. Since God is not a *kind* of being, God is able to be the *source* of all finite being.

As sheer, infinite "to be," God is possessed of all the perfections of infinite being. In this regard, Thomas cites the words of the Prophet Isaiah: "To whom then will you liken God, or what likeness compare with him?" (Is 40:18). God cannot be likened to any finite being because God is infinite, and not on the same ontological plane as creatures. Yet God is not aloof or distant. Actually, if God were just a big finite being, then God could not be close to most finite beings, since he would be separated from them by space, time, and so forth. Precisely because God is infinite being, he is present everywhere intimately.

Thomas teaches that God is one. Here Thomas draws attention to Deuteronomy 6:4, "Hear, O Israel: The Lord our God is one Lord." This passage from Moses' farewell address to Israel became the foundation of the Jewish prayer known as the *Shema*. Since God is pure "to be," pure actuality, God is not one in the sense of "one thing among many things." Rather, God is one in the sense of *undivided and indivisible being*. Thomas describes God's undivided being as utterly "simple," because God is not a composite of anything. God is infinite being, with all the perfections of being, in an infinite mode.

Thomas knows that throughout the New Testament, Jesus is recognized to be the preexisting Son of God, equal to the Father. The Holy Spirit, too, is often presented as a discrete divine agent. How does this not compromise the testimony of Israel's Scriptures that there is only one God? Indebted to Augustine, Thomas takes his cue from the Gospel of John's opening line: "In the beginning was the Word, and the Word was with God, and the Word was God" (Jn 1:1). God and his Word—Father and Son—are the one God, and yet they are distinct. When Thomas asks how this can be, he observes that the Father's generation of a Word can be compared to the mind's generating of an "inner word" or concept. For example, when your mind thinks about and loves itself—when you ponder your mind and think, "I love my mind!"—then the object doing the thinking, and the subject of your thinking, and even the love you have for the subject are all, in fact, your mind. Here we have a creaturely analogy for the divine mystery of three in one.

STRUCTURE *of the* SUMMA THEOLOGIAE

The *Summa theologiae* has been aptly described as "From the Trinity, to the Trinity." Its three parts unfold in a way that traces this journey. The first part explores the divine Trinity, the missions of the Father, Son, and Holy Spirit, the work of creation, and the government of the universe.

The second part examines the human person who desires happiness, the eternal and divine law that shows the path of human flourishing, and the infused and acquired virtues that enable this flourishing in full.

The third part exhibits the unification of the Trinity and humanity in the Person and work of Jesus Christ, who is himself the way for the return of human beings to the Trinity. It also includes discussion of the sacraments.

Each part includes a series of questions and responses. The statement or the question is followed by a list of counter-positions to the one Thomas will take. After the objections, there is a section called *sed contra* ("but on the other hand"), which is a statement by another theologian or philosopher or a scriptural passage that is meant to bolster or illumine Thomas' position. Next, Thomas' formal response to the original question is presented as well as an answer to each of the objections.

This structure mirrors the style and practice of the medieval "disputed questions" forum that was discussed in the video.

QUESTIONS FOR UNDERSTANDING

1. What were the two ways Thomas was a radical of his times? How can being a Christian today also be seen as radical by the culture? (John 15:18-19; Matt 8:21-27; James 4:1-5, 8-10; 1 Pet 4:1-4)

2. What or who is God, according to Christian belief? What does Thomas add to our understanding of God? (Ex 3:14; Isa 40:18; Ps 139:1-18; CCC 213, 230-31, 279, 290, 338)

3. The Church professes and Thomas teaches that "God is one." What does this mean? (Deut 6:4; Isa 44:6; CCC 212-213, 228, 234-37)

4. How is Jesus Christ the fullest revelation of God on earth? (John 1:1-3, 18; Eph 1:15-21; CCC 151, 516, 561, 648)

QUESTIONS FOR APPLICATION

1. When have you experienced a clear sense of mission or purpose that you believe came from God? Did you have obstacles in your way from family or friends, as Thomas did when he joined the Dominicans? If so, how did you respond? If not, where did you find support to follow this mission?

2. How much time do you spend reading, studying, or reflecting on the Bible? How would you respond to St. Jerome's statement, "Ignorance of Scripture is ignorance of Christ"?

3. Thomas strongly believed in open dialogue and discussion of spiritual matters that was inclusive of different opinions. Think about a time when you participated in a discussion about the faith. How did that go? How often do you have those types of discussions? In what ways do you follow your baptismal call to evangelize or "go out and make disciples of all nations"? (Mt 28:19)

4. Near the end of his life, Thomas said that everything he had written "seemed like straw when compared to what has been revealed to me." Reflect and comment on this statement in light of the nature, works, and mystery of God and the nature and works of man.

NOTES:

ST. THOMAS AQUINAS
The Theologian
VIDEO OUTLINE — PART II

I.   FAITH AND REASON

    A. Many philosophers of the time preached that faith and reason were in conflict: if it's true according to faith, then it's false according to reason

    B. Thomas taught that faith and reason are compatible, as they come from the same source: God

    C. Faith is above reason—not opposed to it, but going beyond it. "No sacrifice of the mind is involved in authentic religious faith."

II. THE HUMAN PERSON

    A. Anti-dualist: the unity of the human person; soul and body are one and not opposed to each other

    B. Humans made in the image and likeness of God

    C. Infinite capacity of mind and will

    D. Ordered to something beyond our human nature

III. CHRISTOLOGY

    A. Thomas was deeply in love with Jesus Christ

    B. Supreme act of God's goodness was the Incarnation; God giving himself away

    C. Jesus is the divine ecstasy reaching down and the human ecstasy reaching up, the coming together of divinity and humanity

IV. WHY IS THOMAS A "PIVOTAL PLAYER"?

    A. Showed that faith and reason are not in conflict

    B. Exemplified a true, catholic mind that is open to all influences and not afraid of public, religious discourse

    C. Revealed that God is not competitive with humans

ST. THOMAS AQUINAS

FAITH AND REASON

Some philosophers describe faith as a vice, because they consider "faith" to be belief in something without evidence or even against all evidence. Fortunately, this is not Thomas' understanding of faith. Thomas considers Christian faith to be supported by much evidence. He offers five ways of demonstrating the existence of God. In one of these ways, Thomas begins with the existence of change or motion. When something is changing, this change or motion is caused by something else. In an essentially ordered series of movers, all the movers must exist at the same time in order for the motion to occur, such as a man painting on a canvas. The bristles move the paint, the paintbrush handle moves the bristles, the hand moves the paintbrush handle, the mind moves the hand, etc. All of the movers act simultaneously. If one of the movers stops moving, the whole series stops. Each mover or cause is essential to the result. However, in an accidentally ordered series, the movers do not need to exist at the same time. An example of an accidentally ordered series is the contemporary notion of an infinite series of universes: one universe is caused by another universe that is caused by another universe, and so on infinitely. What Thomas shows is that even such an infinite series of movers is itself a contingent mover, for what causes the motion of the infinite series? (In other words, what caused the infinite series of universes?) There must be a prime mover that is "unmoved," but infinitely in motion.

Although Thomas gives several arguments that demonstrate God's existence, he admits there are reasonable arguments against God's existence. One of them is the prevalence of evil and suffering in our world. How could God permit this? The quandary, however, is hardly an argument that makes belief in God irrational, even though it puts a difficult question to God. God's answer, Thomas makes clear, is found in Jesus Christ, who enters directly into the heart of the evil of suffering and shows God's love and power therein. The answer to evil is love.

Thomas also believes the resurrection of Jesus offers good evidence for God. But how do we know that actually happened? Thomas maintains that it is not irrational to accept the testimony of others for certain beliefs, and the first Christians all testified joyfully to the resurrection of Jesus. God prepared for the coming of Jesus in the centuries that preceded his coming, and the Scriptures of Israel testify to this preparation. Jesus performed miracles, taught with unique authority, and was recognized as a striking figure—indeed was crucified for claiming to be able to do what only God can do. Jesus gathered twelve disciples, upon whom he established his messianic community of love through the power of the Holy Spirit. The Church is this community, as shown by its saints. Of course, the Church is filled with sinners, but the saints show the real power of love.

For all these reasons, faith is most certainly not blind. It is supported by good, rational arguments and logic. Yet Thomas does consider faith to be a gift given to us by God. It is not something we can summon through our own energies. Although the certitude of our faith in Jesus Christ is supported by the evidence, it does not come from it. This is because faith's certitude comes from the Holy Spirit drawing us into relationship with Jesus. Faith is a knowing by which God draws rational creatures into relationship with him. This is why faith always involves interpersonal communion, both with God and with other Christians.

†

THE HUMAN PERSON

Today, the human person is often imagined to be a complex mass of bones, muscles, organs, and nerves, with a complex nervous system and a brain that gives us a sense of an enduring, conscious self and of freedom of thought and action. Thomas was well aware of materialist views of the human person, which try to reduce the entire human experience to basic material explanations. But he argued that such views were insufficient. Take the issue of consciousness, for example. In our minds, we can form the concept of "triangularity"—or the *essence* of a triangle—even though no perfect triangle has ever existed in matter. We've never seen the concept of "triangularity," only particular triangles. Yet if our consciousness were solely material, then our concepts would also have to be material, including our concept of triangularity. But it is not. Therefore, there must be some things, such as abstract concepts like triangularity, that are inexplicable in material terms. This is a strong support for the belief that every person has an immaterial soul, a life-principle within that is more than mere matter.

While affirming the existence of the immaterial soul, Thomas emphasizes that the human person is not a soul that extrinsically uses a body. This notion was already present in Platonism, and it emerged with a vengeance in the mechanistic anthropology of the 17th-century philosopher René Descartes. Cartesian philosophy—philosophy based on Descartes' works—denigrates the body, treating it as the soul's machine. By contrast, for Thomas the soul is the "form" of the body. This does not mean that the soul is the *shape* of the body. Instead it means that everything about the body *is what it is because of* the soul, and the operation of the soul is always intrinsically united to the body. Thomas therefore teaches that in human acts of knowing, images drawn from the senses are always involved. Brain scans that show particular parts of the brain to be at work when we think of particular things are what Thomas would have expected. Indeed, Thomas holds that without the brain's activity, human thinking cannot proceed. The separation of body and soul in death, then, is a radical rupture rather than an escape or a flight of the soul to a higher realm. Although the soul survives death, the soul never loses its radical orientation toward its body. That's why bodily resurrection is so central to Christianity.

Thomas' view of the human person has a major impact, as we would expect, upon his ethics. For Thomas, our bodies are not simply made for our souls to *use*. Rather, because our body and soul constitute a radical unity, our embodied actions must express love. The body, like the soul, has an orientation toward self-giving love. For Thomas, sins against the body are such because they distort the true purposes of our body (as well as our soul). The goodness of the body means that we cannot simply use our bodies for any kinds of acts. Our ensouled bodies are instead made for good acts, acts that express a true gift of self rather than selfish greed or

---

ST. THOMAS AQUINAS: *The Theologian*

the desire to use another person for our purposes and pleasures. This does not mean that Thomas is opposed to bodily pleasure; however, he recognizes that pleasure is an accompaniment of good bodily acts rather than their sole purpose. Indeed, Thomas goes so far as to say that before original sin, humans would have experienced bodily pleasure far more intensely than we do now. Thomas' theology of law and virtue in Christ aims to restore our body-soul activities to the joyful purposes of self-giving love.

Thomas considers that it is specifically the soul that renders the human person the "image of God" (Gen 1:27). Humans are the relational image of God in a way that other animals, despite their goodness, cannot be. This is because humans can know and love God and each other. We have a longing for happiness, which requires an enduring communion with our Creator and friendships with other humans. We want to love forever, and it is for this that we have been created. Sin does not make us happy. Despite its allure, sin isolates us and confines us within ourselves. Since we are made happy by relationships with God and neighbor, we are made uniquely in the image of the triune God, who is communion-in-unity and who rejoices when we share in his goodness.

†

CHRISTOLOGY

Thomas conceives of the Word, Jesus the Son of God, as the perfect expression of the Father, containing all that the Trinity is. The Word expresses not only the Trinity, but also all creatures that God creates out of sheer desire to share his goodness. When God creates human creatures, he wills to share his goodness with us in the highest possible way. The foundation of the Incarnation, then, is the overflowing goodness of God.

In Thomas' view, humans are in great need of the incarnate Word for two reasons. First, we have soiled the image of God in ourselves. We were created to love, but human history is filled with abuse and violence, selfishness and greed. We need to have our "image" restored; and the Word is the true image of the Father. Second, humans are called to a destiny greater than our created powers could ever attain. We were created to share in the divine communion of the Trinity. This is the great tragedy of sin: created to share in the divine life, we instead fall lower than even mere human nature should be. We are bent downwards, unable to raise our minds to the realities for which we were made, and unable to truly see ourselves, others, and God. The Word became flesh, therefore, not only to heal the image of God, but also to elevate the image of God within mankind.

For Thomas, Jesus Christ as the Word incarnate does not simply show up at a random point in history. Rather, he appears only when the love story of God with the human race has been revealed. To show his love in the midst of history, God chose Israel, made a covenant with Israel, and gave Israel a holy and good law. Jesus is born as a member of the people of Israel, and he brings the love story to fulfillment. The Davidic king's job is to make his people just, and, as Thomas shows, Jesus does this on the Cross. By his Resurrection and Ascension, Jesus inaugurates the Kingdom of God and pours forth the holy spirit. He does so in order to reveal and make possible a new way of living in the world, a way of self-sacrificial love rather than self-centered striving.

In his reflection on Jesus' divine and human natures, Thomas emphasizes the unity of Jesus' Person. It is not Jesus' natures—his humanity or his divinity—that do what Jesus does. Rather, it is Jesus Christ, one Person, who does these things. But would not Jesus' two natures come into conflict? When two different natures come together, such as peanut butter and chocolate, they either form a new mixture, with a new nature that is neither peanut butter nor chocolate, or they remain together but with two distinct natures, like a chocolate shell surrounding peanut butter filling. By contrast, because the divine nature is not on the same ontological plane as any creaturely nature, there can be no competition or conflict between the divine nature and the human nature. In prayer, Jesus is fully obedient to the divine will, even when his natural human instinct for self-preservation has to be set aside.

The Incarnation is a Trinitarian action. God sends his Son into the world, and the humanity of the incarnate Son is filled with the Holy Spirit. When Jesus Christ acts to restore and elevate us, this work is Trinitarian in power and has as its goal our eternal sharing in the life of the triune God. Indeed, the Incarnation cannot be separated from Pentecost, when the risen Christ pours out his Spirit upon the gathered apostles. In faith and in the sacraments of the faith, Jesus enables us to share in his saving work and to be united to his Body. In each human life, the incarnate Lord's power in the Holy Spirit is manifested when we act with self-sacrificial love for the good of our neighbor and the glory of our Creator.

TE DEUM TOTIUS CONSOLATIONIS

Hymn written by St. Thomas Aquinas and translated by Gerard Manley Hopkins, S.J.

O God of all consolation, upon Thee I call,
Who seest in us nothing Thou hast not given,
That after the end of this life
Thou might deign to grant the knowledge of Thee, First Truth,
And the fulfillment of Thy divine majesty.

Fill up in my body,
Most bountiful Rewarder,
The beauty of light,
The agility of prompt obedience,
The fine ability to do Thy will,
The strength of indifference to harm.

Add to these
The affluence of Thy riches,
The influx of all delights,
The gathering together of all that is good,

That I may be able to have Thy consolation above me,
The pleasantness of what lies beneath me,
The glorification of body and soul within me,
According to the delightful gathering of Angels
and men about me.

May I obtain with Thee, merciful Father,
The enlightenment of wisdom for my mind,
The hunger for what is truly desirable,
The praise of triumph for my striving,
Where there is, with Thee
The avoidance of all danger,
The many mansions,
Concord of the will,
Where there is [with Thee]
The pleasantness of spring,
The radiance of summer
The fruitfulness of fall,
And the deep sleep of winter.

Grant us, O Lord, God,
Life without death,
Joy without sorrow,
Where there is
The fullness of Liberty,
Boundless security,
Secure tranquility,
Merry happiness,
Joyful eternity,
Eternal blessedness,
Vision of Truth and praise, O God. Amen.

ST. THOMAS AQUINAS: *The Theologian*

1. How would Thomas and the Church answer those who believe that faith and reason are incompatible? (CCC 154-159, 286)

2. Describe what the soul is and how it relates to the human body. How should we treat the body based on this understanding? (Gen 2:7; Eccles 12:7; CCC 33, 362-366, 382)

3. What does it mean to be "made in the image and likeness of God"? How has sin changed that and what restores it? (Gen 1:26; CCC 356-57; Rom 3:23; CCC 2809; CCC 705, 1701-02)

4. In Thomas' view, humans are in great need of the incarnate Word. Who is the incarnate Word and why do we need him? (John 1:1-4; CCC 241-42; Acts 4:10-12; John 14:6-7; Matt 1:21; CCC 1741)

QUESTIONS FOR APPLICATION

1. The story is told that Thomas put his treatise on the Eucharist at the foot of the Cross, asking for guidance. Christ spoke from the Cross, telling Thomas he had written well and asking what he would like in return. What would you answer if Christ said, "What do you want me to give you?" What do you think Thomas was requesting when he said, "*Nothing but you, Lord*"?

2. Are you in love with Jesus? If so, describe that love. If not, reflect and comment on whether you'd like to be in love with him. How can we fall in love more deeply or grow closer to Jesus during our lives here on earth?

3. Why are you Catholic? Please incorporate your understanding of faith and reason in your answer.

NOTES:

ST. CATHERINE *of* SIENA

The Mystic

CATHOLICISM
THE PIVOTAL PLAYERS
VOLUME I

St. Catherine of Siena Study Guide written by Fr. Paul Murray, O.P.

ST. CATHERINE of SIENA
The Mystic

STUDY GUIDE WRITTEN BY
Fr. Paul Murray, O.P.

Fr. Paul Murray, O.P. is an Irish Dominican priest, a poet, and a professor at the Angelicum, the Pontifical University of St. Thomas in Rome. Drawn to what Hans Urs von Balthasar calls "theology on its knees," he has been greatly influenced by the writings of St. Catherine of Siena, St. John of the Cross, and St. Teresa of Avila.

Fr. Murray is the author of several books which have been published in Ireland, England, and the United States including *A Journey with Jonah* (Columba Press, 2002), *The New Wine of Dominican Spirituality* (Burnes & Oates, 2006), and *Scars* (Bloomsbury Academic, 2014). He lives in Rome and is well known as a speaker throughout the United States.

ST. CATHERINE *of* SIENA
The Mystic
VIDEO OUTLINE — PART I

I.   INTRODUCTION
- A. Fascinating Catherine: uneducated; counselor to popes and kings; Doctor of the Church
- B. Mystical power vs. worldly definition of power

II.   LIFE AND TIMES
- A. Her vision as a young girl
- B. Vow of virginity and living as a recluse
- C. Mantellate/Order of Dominicans
- D. Motif in writings: blood

III.   AVIGNON
- A. Papacy in exile in Avignon
- B. Convinced Pope Gregory XI to return to Rome from Avignon
- C. Supported Urban VI, Gregory's successor

IV.   CATHERINE'S UNDERSTANDING OF GOD
- A. Named Doctor of the Church
- B. God is beauty, truth, and love itself
- C. God is "crazy in love" with the world

THE LIFE & TEACHING *of* ST. CATHERINE *of* SIENA

Catherine of Siena is the only lay woman ever proclaimed a Doctor of the Church. For most of her life, except when she was away on a mission of one kind or another, she stayed at home with her family in Siena. Born on March 25, 1347, she died at the age of 33 on April 29, 1380. One of the closest friends of Catherine most affected by her death was a young Sienese poet, Neri dei Pagliaresi. A single stanza from the elegy he wrote at the time of her death offers a vivid, intimate portrait of his much-missed friend:

> Tell me, who will save me now from an evil end?
>
> Who will preserve me from delusions?
>
> Who will guide me when I try to climb?
>
> Who will console me now in my distress?
>
> Who will ask me now: "Are you not well?"
>
> Who will persuade me that I shall not be damned?[1]

ST. CATHERINE'S "LIVING VOICE"

What Catherine of Siena was clearly able to communicate, again and again to the many friends and associates who surrounded her during her short life, was an extraordinary sense of their own human dignity and worth. This was due, in part, to the profundity of her message—to the grace of the Gospel itself. But it was also related to the remarkable instinct she possessed for delivering a word of encouragement—a straightforward, illuminating word—just when it was needed. A measure of the strength of Catherine's personality and character is that, even today, a clear impression of her spirit still survives in her writings and survives, in particular, in the many letters she wrote or dictated: "I Catherine, servant and slave of God's servants, am writing to *encourage* you...."[2] Catherine writes, at times, with the warmth and loving audacity of a girl-child; at other times, with all the power and passion of an Old Testament prophet: "Let it not seem hard to you if I pierce you with the words which the love of your salvation has made me write; rather would I pierce you with my living voice, did God permit it."[3]

Catherine of Siena was a young lay woman without an official role or title within the Church, and yet she did not hesitate to write or dictate letters to all kinds of people: cardinals, monks, family members, nuns, hermits, widows, priests, a mercenary soldier, a king, a tyrant, a queen, a prostitute, a lawyer, a poet, and—amazing to recall—two Roman Pontiffs, Gregory XI and Urban VI. Reading her work today, we cannot help but wonder what it must have been like to meet her in person. Blessed Raymond of Capua, her great friend and spiritual director, the man who knew her perhaps better than anyone else, tells us that even though Catherine's writings are indeed remarkable, they must take "second place" to what he calls "her living words as they came from her lips during her lifetime."[4] He writes: "For the Lord had endowed her with a most ready tongue, a charisma of utterance adapted to every circumstance, so that her words burnt like a torch and none who ever heard her could escape being touched."[4] And there was something else as well about Catherine which, Raymond admits, can hardly be put into words. He writes:

> My heart overflows as I recall it, and compels me to record here this mysterious attraction which was part of her. It made itself felt, not only by her spoken word, but by the very fact of one being present where she was. By it she drew the souls of men to the things of God, and made them take delight in God himself. She drove out despondency from the hearts of any who shared her company, and banished dejection of spirit and all

feelings of depression, bringing in instead a peace of soul so deep that those who experienced it did not know themselves.[6]

†

ST. CATHERINE IN CONTEXT: LIFE AND TIMES

Catherine was an exuberant child, fond of play and adventure. However at an early age, she felt drawn to devote herself entirely to Christ. At the age of eighteen, she joined a lay Dominican group of women called the *Mantellate*. This choice for a Dominican way of life—a Dominican association—is worth noting. Catherine's childhood and adolescence were spent in close proximity to the hugely impressive Dominican church in Siena, and this early contact with the Dominican friars would come, in time, to exercise a profound influence on the development of her own spirituality.

†

A CONTEMPLATIVE IN THE WORLD

As a member of the *Mantellate*, Catherine resolved to pursue a life of prayer and contemplation, choosing for the next three years to remain at home in her parents' house, but living as a recluse. One of the great and saving truths about God's nature that came home forcibly to Catherine during this time was the astonishing fact that God had loved us first, a love that was unconditional. "I loved you without being loved by you, even before you existed."[7] Catherine wanted very much to respond to God with something of the same generous, unconditional love, but how was such a thing to be achieved? The answer, she discovered, was in choosing to love her neighbors as she had been loved by God, serving the needs of both friends and enemies with a devoted, unconditional love—"loving them without being loved by them in return."[8]

For the next three years after her reclusive period, Catherine spent a considerable part of the day out in the streets of Siena, caring for the sick and the needy, the poor, and the afflicted—attending to Christ in his hidden disguise with the same undistracted energy she had devoted to the task of solitude. At first, however, Catherine was not wholly convinced about this call to a new life of active service, fearing that the contact she enjoyed with God in contemplative solitude might somehow be lost. But Christ answered Catherine's fears with these great words of reassurance:

> I have no intention whatever of parting you from myself, but rather of making sure to bind you to me all the closer by the bond of your love for your neighbor. Remember that I have laid down two commandments of love: love of me and love of your neighbor... On two feet you must walk my way, on two wings you must fly to heaven.[9]

With Catherine's attention powerfully redirected by this apostolic imperative, much of her time was spent, according to Blessed Raymond, "in the give and take of social intercourse." But people questioned her motives. "They said of her: 'Why is that one gadding about so much? She's a woman. Why doesn't she stay in her cell if it's God she wants to serve?' "[10] Even Raymond may have reproached Catherine for her boundless apostolic energy and for the kind of company she kept as a result. In any case, Catherine felt it necessary to reveal to him what she called her "secret," telling him how, lifted up in an ecstasy like Saint Paul on one occasion, she saw "the secret things of God, things which it is not given to any pilgrim here below to utter."[11]

During the ecstasy, Catherine's first thought was that she had attained to heaven and would remain there in bliss forever. But her "Eternal Spouse" said to her: "You must go back; the salvation of many souls demands it. It demands, too, a radical change in the way of life that has been yours up to this. Your cell [the room in her house at Siena] will no longer be your dwelling place.... You will even have to leave your own city. But I will be with you always."[12] After this time, Catherine's only consolation in life, her only joy, was in seeking out the lost. She said to Raymond: "Father, now that I have let you into my secret I know it will keep you from ever taking part with those who denounce me for that openness of spirit with which I freely welcome all the souls who come my way."[13]

✝

THE CHURCH OF HER TIME

As her fame for holiness increased, Catherine found herself drawn into some of the most pressing affairs of the Church and also into the murky drama of Italian politics. During the years 1375-78, for example, there was the fierce conflict between Florence and the Holy See. Then directly afterwards, threatening the very survival of the papacy, came the Great Western Schism (see sidebar). Although these particular dramas obviously belong to a time and place utterly remote from the specific dramas of our own century, certain aspects of the world into which Catherine was born bear a striking resemblance to the situation in which we find ourselves today.

For a start, the time span of Catherine's life was marked by enormous change and upheaval, both within the Church and in society in general. An old world was disappearing fast, the world of the Middle Ages, and what the future might bring was by no means clear. Catherine's contemporaries witnessed the damage caused by wars and by countless natural disasters, but witnessed also the truly terrifying horror of the Black Death (the bubonic plague). The plague succeeded in decimating almost two-thirds of Europe's population. At the same time, a different kind of plague was at work within the Church, a plague of unbelievable corruption. Catherine felt constrained, as a result, to acknowledge that the Church she loved so deeply had become "a garden overgrown with putrid flowers,"[14] a bride whose "face is disfigured with leprosy."[15]

Not least among the scandals in the Church at that time was that the pope, instead of living close to his own flock in the diocese of Rome, was residing at Avignon in France. Catherine knew that this long, drawn-out absence on the part of the Bishop of Rome was causing untold harm to the Church and to society at large. She wrote to Pope Gregory XI and traveled to Avignon to implore him to return to Rome. Her letters to the pope, appealing to him to return to the See of Rome, are memorable for the note of childlike warmth and intimacy with which she addresses him, not hesitating now and again to call him "Daddy" (*babbo*). But the letters are also notable for the peremptory tone adopted by Catherine, speaking to the pope on occasion more as a prophet than a girl-child:

> Up, father, courageously! I tell you, you have no need to fear. But if you don't do as you should, you may well have reason to be afraid. It is your duty to come. So come! Come trustingly, without any fear at all.[16]

And again:

> Let us go quickly, my dear *babbo*, and fearlessly! If God is for you, no one will be against you. God himself will move you; God himself will be your guide, your helmsman, and your sailor.[17]

This last letter was written in the summer of 1376. A mere six months later, much to Catherine's delight, the pope returned to Rome. Centuries later, Pope Benedict XVI, commenting on the contribution made to the Church by people like Catherine, remarked: "How could we imagine the government of the Church without this contribution, which sometimes becomes very visible, such as when Saint Hildegard criticized the bishops, or when Saint Bridget offered recommendations and Saint Catherine of Siena obtained the return of the popes to Rome?"[18] The nature of Catherine's contribution to the Church on this occasion, her inspired intervention, belongs to what Pope Benedict calls the "charismatic sector" within the Church—as distinct from "the ministerial sector."[19] It is in fact a necessary form of contribution, one which, in Pope Benedict's opinion, is "always a crucial factor without which the Church cannot survive."[20]

One of the ironies of Catherine's life is that the return of the pope to Rome helped precipitate the tragedy of the Great Western Schism in ways that could never have been foreseen or imagined. To Catherine's enormous distress, after the death of Pope Gregory and very soon after the election of a new pope, Urban VI, the Church found itself divided into two warring factions with two claimants to the Chair of Peter. No event in ecclesial life could have wounded Catherine more deeply. It was a tragedy that marked the few remaining years of her life.

That said, Catherine never for a moment lost her confidence in Christ's power to protect his Church, even from the worst of enemies—in this case, a group of self-serving cardinals who had sided with the antipope Clement VII. In a letter to His Holiness, Pope Urban VI, she wrote: "There is nothing—no difficulty, no sort of trouble—that can overcome you.... The blows of wretched, wicked, self-centered people will not harm your soul's will. Nor will they topple holy Church, the bride; she cannot fail, because she is founded on the living Rock, Christ gentle Jesus."[21] Although utterly exhausted and near death, Catherine spent the last weeks of her life praying in Saint Peter's Basilica for Church reform and for Church unity. She died on April 29, 1380, invoking over and over again the mercy of Christ's saving blood.

Catherine of Siena's short life, viewed now in retrospect, appears to be an extraordinary mixture of success and failure. Her role in securing the return of the pope to Rome was, for a young woman of that period, quite a remarkable achievement, as was the impact she had on so many of her contemporaries. Nevertheless, Catherine was by no means successful in all her endeavors. For example, her plan for a "papal council" of holy men advising the pope came to nothing. Also, quite a few of her attempts to bring peace between warring factions in Italy betrayed more innocent naiveté than political astuteness. Given these facts, it's clear that Catherine's legacy should not be looked for in the social or political sphere, but rather in that passionate and lucid body of teaching that has come down to us in her writings, in her letters, in her prayers, and in her "book," now popularly known as *The Dialogue*. Full ecclesial recognition of the importance of these writings came on October 4, 1970, when Pope Paul VI declared Catherine to be a Doctor of the Church, giving her the highest status possible among the Church's most celebrated authors and theologians.

THE GREAT WESTERN SCHISM

While St. Catherine was successful in convincing Pope Gregory XI to leave Avignon and return to Rome, the unity of the Church under one pope only lasted a short time.

Gregory XI died less than two years after returning to Rome, and the College of Cardinals elected Pope Urban VI in April 1378. For six months, there was not a single objection to the election of Urban VI, even among the French church.

However, Pope Urban did not get along well with the cardinals that had elected him, often acting in a haughty and suspicious way. There are historical reports that he also blatantly criticized these cardinals, sometimes without cause. Many of the cardinals, comfortable with the power and support of the French government, wanted to move the papacy back to Avignon. Urban VI strongly opposed leaving Rome, and this added to the tension.

Catherine tirelessly supported Pope Urban, as she believed he was the legitimately elected successor to the Chair of Peter. She even lived in Rome at the pope's request for the rest of her short life. However, in her truthful and courageous way, she encouraged Urban VI to work more harmoniously with the cardinals that had elected him.

The Schism began when the same 13 cardinals, unhappy with the temperament and actions of Urban VI, met in September 1378 and elected a new pope. Ignoring Urban VI's legitimacy, they installed Robert of Geneva, who took the name of Clement VII. Again, Catherine was openly critical of the cardinals in their revolt against Urban VI, whom they had previously elected. Some months later, Clement VII was driven out of Italy and took up residence in Avignon. The Schism was now firmly established and would last for 40 years.

Clement VII was well connected with the key European royal families and was politically skilled and influential. The Church was divided and the faithful generally followed the opinion of their countries and secular rulers in choosing between the two popes.

The rival popes excommunicated each other and created new groups of cardinals to lobby on their behalf throughout the Christian world. St. Catherine passed away in 1380, followed by Urban's death in 1389. In Rome, Boniface IX succeeded Urban VI and in Avignon, Benedict XIII succeeded Clement VII after his death.

In the early 15th century, the King of France lost faith in Benedict and released his people from obedience to him. He also set up a blockade of Avignon to cut him off from his supporters. Benedict refused to submit but was deposed in 1417.

In 1414, the Council of Constance was formed and prioritized unity within the Church above all else. In 1417, a united conclave representing all the nations and coming directly out of the Council, elected Martin V, who was installed in Rome. The Great Western Schism was finally ended.

However, the Schism did have repercussions. Some scholars believe that the division in the Church greatly harmed the papacy and helped fuel the Protestant Reformation.

QUESTIONS FOR UNDERSTANDING

1. What evidence do we have that God loved us first, and loves us unconditionally? (CCC 270, 315, 545; Ps 145:8-19; Jn 3:16-17; Luke 15:3-7)

2. How should we love God? (Deut 6:4-7; Matt 22:37-40; John 13:34; CCC 1822-23, 1878, 2093; 1 John 4:19-21)

3. In what ways did St. Catherine follow the commandment to "love one
    another" during her life on earth? What are the characteristics of this
    type of love? (CCC 1825, 2443-44, 2447; 1 Corinthians 13:4-7)

4. St. Catherine talked and wrote much about the blood of Christ; in
    fact, she repeated the word "blood" over and over at her death. What
    is significant about blood in the Old Covenant? How does blood
    relate to the New Covenant? (Gen 15:7-12, 17-18; Ex 24:3-8; Lev 17:11;
    Heb 9:12-14, 22; Lk 22:19-20; CCC 613, 1365)

QUESTIONS FOR APPLICATION

1. In looking back over St. Catherine's life, it is interesting that her time was very balanced between contemplative prayer and service. Jesus sent her on mission through prayer, and it seemed she did not go where he did not lead her. How would you characterize the balance of prayer and action in your life? Does prayer precede your works of mercy? How can you be sure that you are doing the works that God wants you to do and not those that, in your own ego, you believe are necessary?

2. St. Catherine experienced continual encounters with Christ. When and how have you encountered Christ in your life? How did that change your attitude and behavior? What mission is Christ asking of you now and in the near future?

ST. CATHERINE *of* SIENA
The Mystic
VIDEO OUTLINE — PART II

I. SIN AND SALVATION
- A. Metaphor of the raging river of sin and the bridge, who is Christ
- B. Moving from the river up three steps to unity with the divine
  1. Reject sin due to fear of punishment (feet of Christ)
  2. Reject sin due to love of God, but value his consolations more than God himself (heart of Christ)
  3. Reject sin due to filial love as son or daughter of God (mouth of Christ)
- C. Love of God inextricably linked to love of neighbor
- D. Tears of people
  1. Bitter tears of those condemned to hell
  2. Fearful tears of beginners in faith
  3. Tender tears of those beginning to fall in love with God
  4. Perfect tears of those in union with God
  5. Sweet tears of those who have utterly surrendered to God

II. COOPERATING WITH GRACE
- A. God gives us grace first and we are called to cooperate with it
- B. Self awareness
- C. Refrain from judgment of others
- D. Pray and work for salvation of all
- E. Never seek reward for our love
- F. Dedicated prayer life
- G. Take up the cross of Christ
  1. Union with God is best accomplished by communion with Christ
  2. Getting rid of self-love always involves suffering

III. VISIONS AND ECSTASIES
  A. The more you have Christ, the more you want him
  B. Goal is total union of the human and divine will
  C. Catherine did not dwell on her visions or ecstasies and told all not to seek them

IV.. CATHERINE AS "PIVOTAL PLAYER"
  A. Witness to the dimension beyond this world
  B. Intensity of her love; a conduit of grace and love to this world

ST. CATHERINE *of* SIENA: MYSTIC

What kind of theologian was Catherine of Siena? Generally speaking, Doctors of the Church are not only saints but brilliant intellectuals, people who have received, from an early age, a broad academic education. In the case of Catherine, however, it was quite late in her life that she learned to read, and even then she read with great difficulty. Her theology was acquired not by academic learning but rather by a unique mystical grace, something underlined by Pope Paul VI when he declared her a Doctor of the Church:

> What strikes us most about the saint is her infused wisdom; that is, her lucid, profound, and inebriating absorption of the divine truths and mysteries of the faith... That assimilation was certainly favored by singular natural gifts, but it was also evidently...due to a mystic charism.[22]

Like any other theologian, Catherine presents and explores the great truths of the Christian faith in her writings. Her teaching, however, tends to assume the form of ardent exhortation rather than dogged and detailed exposition. She is clearly not a scholastic theologian. For all her brilliance, Catherine comes across as more of an apostle than an intellectual, more of a preacher than a scholar. If it should occur to us to think of Catherine in relation to a text such as the *Summa* of Saint Thomas Aquinas, her work—the text of her life—is like a *Summa* set on fire, her writings characterized not by academic speculation but rather by a passionate and anguished concern for the salvation of the world.

The eternal Father to Catherine: "Do you know, daughter, who you are and who I am? If you know these two things you will have beatitude within your grasp. You are she who is not, and I AM HE WHO IS."
- Blessed Raymond of Capua, *Life of Catherine of Siena, 92*

"We've been deceived by the thought that we would be more pleasing to God in our own way than in the way God has given us." - Letter T340

Generally speaking, we regard Christian mystics as men and women who possess an intimate knowledge of the higher states and stages of the spiritual life. We don't tend to think of them as dedicated preachers of the Gospel. That's why it will no doubt come as a surprise, for some readers, to learn that Catherine of Siena was one of the greatest preachers of the Good News in the entire Christian tradition. One can find in her work some quite remarkable descriptions of her own contemplative union with God. But the principal concern of Catherine was not to speak of such experiences, but rather to draw attention to the astonishing power, love, and beauty of God himself. That is her obsessive theme—the core subject of the Good News—to which she returns again and again in her writings.

Here, for example, is a characteristic extract from one of Catherine's prayers in which, with manifest amazement, she contemplates the marvel of God's compassionate nature:

> O ineffable love, although in your light you saw all the iniquities which your creature would commit against your infinite goodness, you acted as if you did not see; rather, you kept your eye on the beauty of your creature with whom you had fallen in love, like one drunk and crazy with love, and through love you drew her from yourself and gave her being.[23]

In a similar vein at one point in *The Dialogue*, finding herself overwhelmed by the thought of God's extraordinary goodness, she exclaims: "O eternal Father... O eternal beauty... O eternal mercy! O hope and refuge of sinners!... O mad lover!...Why then are you so mad? Because you have fallen in love with what you have made."[24]

APOSTLE OF FREEDOM

All through her life, Catherine of Siena contemplated God and the nature of God. But in her short life, to a degree almost unique among Christian saints and mystics, Catherine also contemplated human nature, in both its misery and its grandeur. The gift of freedom—freedom to act, freedom to think—constituted for her the greatest mark of our human dignity. Needless to say, then, any loss of that dignity Catherine regarded as an unspeakable tragedy. Nothing distressed her more, in fact, than the sight of free men and women reduced by the pressure of their own weakness, or by the environment in which they lived, to a debilitating moral servitude. Almost every page of her writing is, as a result, an impassioned manifesto of freedom.

Writing to a friend on one occasion, she exclaims: "What is this thing that is ours, given us by God, that neither the devil nor anyone else can take from us?" And she replies: "It is our will."[25] And again in another place, she writes: "No one can force us to commit the slightest sin, because God has put *yes* and *no* into the strongest thing there is, into our will."[26] Here Catherine is paying us an enormous compliment as human beings. But Catherine is not naive. She knows full well that our nature has been weakened since the Fall, and that all too easily "we lose our mastery and become the servants and slaves of sin."[27] But even if reduced by weakness, we should take heart, Catherine advises, and run to God as a child runs to its mother, with a child's bold confidence, bringing all our fears and all our knowledge of weakness and failure into God's presence. Love—the "wondrous charity" of God, Catherine explains—is the "gentlest of mothers." It is the "remedy for all our weakness."[28] So she writes: "Stay near your gentle mother, charity, who will free you from all servile fear and give you strength, magnanimity, and freedom of heart."[29]

Catherine's overriding concern in making such statements is to lead people from fear into freedom. She knows that fear can assume many different forms: fear of what people think of us or how they judge us, fear of death and suffering, fear of God's judgment, fear even of ourselves, of our own weakness. Catherine's teaching on how best to respond to such fears finds memorable expression in a letter she sent to a married woman named Costanza Soderini. The relevant passage in the letter begins:

> Sometimes people suffer a great deal from fear of death because of their self-indulgence. The first is a delusion the devil puts in their minds. He says, "You see that you are going to die, and that you haven't done a bit of good! So do you know where you're going? Your deeds have earned only hell!" On the other hand, he makes them feel sorry for themselves by saying, "Just think! Your body is so pampered now with worldly pleasures, but soon you will die."[30]

The devil, Catherine explains, exploits the deepest human fears in order to lead people into "discouragement and despair." "He wants them to see only their shortcomings and sins, and to hide the divine mercy from them."[31] So how, then, are we to respond? Catherine's answer reveals two things: first, how sharp is her grasp of human psychology and, second, how profound is her understanding of the nature of God's mercy. She writes:

> We have to counter the devil's great malice by responding to these interior suggestions of his. Turning our gaze to our Creator, we should say, "I acknowledge that I am mortal, but this is a tremendous grace for me, since death will bring me to my goal, to God who is my life. I acknowledge, too, that my life and deeds deserve only hell. But I have faith and trust in my Creator, in the blood of the Lamb who was slain and consumed, that he will pardon my sins and grant me grace. I will try in this present time to amend my life. But if death should overtake me before I have amended my life— that is, before I have yet done penance for my sins—I [still] say that I trust in *Domine nostro Jesu Christo*, because I see that there is no comparison between my sins and divine mercy. Even if all the sins that could possibly be committed were gathered together in one person, it would be like a drop of vinegar in the sea."[32]

ST. CATHERINE'S THREE STATES *of the* SOUL

Describing her communication with God in her book *The Dialogue*, Saint Catherine writes about the stages of spiritual growth using a metaphor of a raging river and a bridge that lifts you above the river and allows safe passage across.

The raging river represents the sinful and fallen world, while the bridge represents Jesus Christ, the way to be free from sin and safely cross into eternal life. Our souls are forced to live in the raging river due to Original Sin and earthly lives lived in a fallen world. Our sole hope for salvation is to climb onto the bridge, to enter into the Divine Life of God's only Son, Jesus Christ.

There are three steps leading up to the bridge of life. The first step, representing most beginners in the spiritual journey, is climbed by the soul desiring to be saved because of its "slavish fear." Catherine quotes God saying: *"The law of fear was the Old Law that I gave to Moses. It was built on fear alone: whoever sinned suffered the penalty. Their slavish fear is not enough to win them eternal life."*

The soul who progresses in faith will next climb the second step, which leads it to reject sin due to its love of God. Catherine describes hearing God say: *The law of love is the New Law given by the Word, my only Begotten Son. The Old Law was not dissolved by the New, but fulfilled. The imperfectness of the fear of suffering was taken away by love, and what remained was the perfectness of holy fear, that is, fear simply of sinning, not because of personal damnation but because sin is an insult to me, supreme Goodness.*

However, a soul's love and charity toward its neighbor on this second step is imperfect, as the person loves *"for their own profit or for the delight and pleasure"* found in God. As long as these souls are receiving blessings, they continue to love. Once those blessings stop, they slip back into the raging river.

To ascend to the third step, souls must *"seek perfect knowledge of themselves so that they will know that of themselves they have neither existence nor any grace."* In challenging times these souls, in true humility, will seek God alone and know him as their "benefactor" and eternal Father. As souls persevere in eliminating all slavish fear and selfish desires, they reach the bridge, attaining true unity with the Trinity in "filial love"—the love of a child for his parent or of God for his children, adopted through Christ.

†

ST. CATHERINE ON PRAYER

QUOTES ON
Prayer

"You are asking for something that would be harmful to your salvation if you had it—so by not getting what you've asked, you really are getting what you want."
- Letter T266

"Oh gentleness of love! How can your bride's heart keep from loving you...?"[33] That short explosion of praise and gratitude occurs in one of Catherine's letters. There are many similar "explosions" in Catherine's writing, moments when, for the space of a phrase or a sentence or even a whole paragraph, Catherine is so struck by the thought of God's love that she is stunned into prayer. Like almost no other saint that comes to mind, her thoughts and feelings seem to catch fire with sheer wonder. She is, to borrow a phrase from the modern poet Mary Oliver, "a bride married to amazement."[34] To her friend and spiritual director, Raymond of Capua, Catherine wrote: "Let our hearts explode wide open, then, as we contemplate a flame and fire of love so great that God has engrafted himself into us and us into himself! O unimaginable love!"[35]

Here what compels Catherine's wonder is the mystery of the Incarnation. But when at prayer, an even greater source of wonder for Catherine is the mystery of our redemption, the mystery of the Cross. For nothing on earth seemed to move her so much as the thought of the blood of the Lamb poured out for us on the Cross. Thus, on one occasion, meditating on the Passion and Death of Christ Jesus, she boldly says:

> "Oh my Lord, what a grace it would have been for me if
> I had been some of the stone or soil in which your cross
> was set, for I would have received some of your blood
> that flowed down from the cross!" Gentle First Truth
> answered: "My dearest daughter, you *were* the stone that
> held me, you and everyone else—I mean my love for
> you—for nothing else could have held me there."[36]

A key aspect of St. Catherine's prayer life is described on one of the first pages of her *Dialogue*. Catherine wrote that on one occasion, lifting up her mind and heart to the Father in prayer and contemplating "the effect of his fiery and consuming love," Catherine discovered not only a vision of God and a vision of herself in God, but also a new and

22

©2016 Word on Fire Catholic Ministries

compassionate vision and understanding of her neighbor. "The love the soul sees that God has for her, she in turn extends to all other creatures. And what is more, she immediately feels compelled to love her neighbor as herself, for she sees how supremely she herself is loved by God, beholding herself in the wellspring of the sea of the divine essence."[37]

Here it becomes clear that Catherine's contemplative experiences are at the core of her deep respect for the individual person. What Catherine receives when at prayer is not simply the command from God to love her neighbor, but an unforgettable insight beyond the symptoms of human distress, a glimpse into the hidden grace and dignity of each person. So deeply affected was Catherine by this vision of her neighbor that she remarked on one occasion to Raymond of Capua that if he could only see this beauty—the inner, hidden beauty—of the individual person as she saw it, he would be willing to suffer and die for it.

During her hours of prayer, God also made Catherine aware of the desperate plights of many of her contemporaries. This fact helps explain why so much of Catherine's prayer life takes the form of intense and continual intercession on behalf of those most in need of mercy. "[Lord], I plead with you: have mercy on the world and restore the warmth of charity and peace and unity to holy Church. I beg you, let your infinite goodness force you not to close the eye of your mercy!"[38]

Because of the many extraordinary gifts Catherine of Siena possessed during her life—gifts of healing, of "reading souls," of extreme fasting, and of receiving private visions and revelations—we might expect to find a marked emphasis on such extraordinary, charismatic phenomena throughout her work. But while never dismissing these things out of hand, Catherine teaches and insists on the *ordinary* way of Christian faith and love. Thus, on the tendency to focus too much attention on special mystical feelings or experiences in prayer, she writes: "Light seems to be failing us, dazzled as we are by our consolations and the hope we place in revelations—things that do not let us know the truth properly, although we may be acting in good faith."[39]

The message is clear. Instead of relying on mere private, subjective experience, we are asked to focus attention on the reality of Christ, the Incarnate Word, and on the liberating objectivity of Christ's teaching.

There are, of course, real contemplative graces, but the bridge that unites us with the Father is not some interior mystical sensation but rather the astonishing sacrificial love of Christ Jesus.

On one of the rare occasions in *The Dialogue* when Catherine turns her attention directly to Christ in prayer, she exclaims: "O mad lover! It was not enough for you to take on our humanity: You had to die as well!"[40] For Catherine, this summarizes the hope for all of us. It is a hope realized already in Christ, in the magnanimity and "madness" of his love: "For he loved us without being loved. Out of love he created us, and then created us anew to grace in his blood. He gave his life with such blazing love."[41]

QUESTIONS FOR UNDERSTANDING

1. What can the life of St. Catherine teach about God's purpose for each person and how to cooperate with his plan? (Jer 29:11; Psalm 139:1-16; CCC 898-900, 1877, 2712, 2724, 2745)

2. How did St. Catherine "witness to a dimension beyond this world" while she was on Earth? (CCC 955-957, 2683; Ephesians 6:10-13)

3. Define and explain what St. Catherine was referring to when she said, "What is this thing that is ours, given us by God, that neither the devil nor anyone else can take from us?" (Sir 15: 11-20; CCC 1730-31)

4. Explain St. Catherine's metaphor about the raging river and the bridge, including the three stages of spiritual growth. (CCC 1852-53; John 14:6; 1 John 4:17-18)

QUESTIONS FOR APPLICATION

1. Reflect on St. Catherine's comment that there is "no comparison between my sins and God's mercy." How can this statement give you hope? What can you do to reap the benefits of God's mercy?

2. Do you ever focus on your feelings and emotions regarding the Faith instead of the reality and truth of Christ and his teachings? How can you become more grounded in Christ and the reality of his teachings and rely less on "interior sensations"?

3. Put yourself into St. Catherine's metaphor (Q. 4 above). Where are you: in the river, on the bridge, or on one of the steps up to the bridge? What is needed for you to progress to the next level?

ENDNOTES

† PART I

1) Cited in Arrigo Levasti, *My Servant, Catherine*, trans. D.M. White (London, 1954), 110.

2) Catherine of Siena to Frate Bartolomeo Domenici, T 200, *The Letters of Saint Catherine of Siena*, trans. S. Noffke (Tempe, AZ: 2000), 1:21.

3) Letter to Three Italian Cardinals, T 310, *Selected Letters of Caterina Benincasa*, trans., by V. D. Scudder (New York 1927) p. 283.

4) Raymond of Capua, *The Life of Catherine of Siena*, trans. C. Kearns (Wilmington, DE: 1980), 8.

5) Ibid.

6) Ibid., 28

7) Catherine, *The Dialogue*, 89, trans. S. Noffke (New York: 1980), 165.

8) Ibid.

9) Raymond, *Life of Catherine*, 139.

10) Ibid, 339.

11) Ibid., 202.

12) Ibid., 204-5.

13) Ibid., 205.

14) Catherine of Siena, *Il Dialogo*, 122, ed. G. Cavallini (Rome: 1968), 306.

15) Ibid., 14, 37-8.

16) Catherine to Pope Gregory XI, T 233, *The Letters of Saint Catherine of Siena*, trans. S. Noffke (Tempe, Arizona: 2001), 2:213.

17) Catherine to Pope Gregory, T 231, *Letters of Saint Catherine*, 2:217.

18) Pope Benedict XVI, "Meeting with Members of the Roman Clergy," Hall of Blessings, Thursday, March 2, 2006.

19) Ibid.

20) Ibid.

21) Catherine to Pope Urban VI, T 306, *The Letters of Saint Catherine of Siena*, trans. S. Noffke (Tempe, AZ: 2007), 3:283.

† PART II

22) Pope Paul VI, "Saint Catherine, Doctor of the Church," *L'Osservatore Romano* 42, 133 (October 15, 1970), 6, AAS LXII, 10, 1970.

23) Catherine, Prayer 4, *S. Caterina Da Siena: Le Orationi*, ed. G. Cavallini (Rome 1978), 46.

24) Catherine, *Dialogue*, 153, p. 325.

25) Catherine to Monna Bartolomea, T 165, *Letters of Saint Catherine*, 2:40.

26) Catherine to Bernabò Visconti, T 28, *Letters of Saint Catherine*, 1:133.

27) Catherine to Sano di Maco, T 69, *Letters of Saint Catherine*, 1:66.

28) Catherine to Bishop Angelo Ricasoli, T 88, *Le Lettere di S. Caterina da Siena*, ed. Misciatelli (Florence: 1940), 2:77-78.

29) Ibid., 79-80.

30) Catherine to Costanza Soderini, T 314, *Letters of Saint Catherine*, 2:486.

31) Ibid.

32) Ibid.

33) Catherine to the Sisters of the Monastery of Santa Maria delle Vergini, T 217, *Letters of Saint Catherine*, 2:562.

34) Mary Oliver, "When Death Comes," *New and Selected Poems* (Boston: 1992), 10.

35) Catherine to Raymond of Capua, T 226, *Letters of Saint Catherine*, 2:6.

36) Catherine to Cardinal Orsini, T 223, *Letters of Saint Catherine*, 1:161-162.

37) Catherine to Raymond, T 226, *Le Lettere di S. Caterina da Siena*, (Florence: 1940), 3:297.

38) Catherine, Prayer 5, *The Prayers of Catherine of Siena*, trans. S. Noffke (New York: 2001), 48.

39) Vol V, ed., P. Misciattelli (Florence 1940) p.79.

40) *The Dialogue*, 30, p.72.

41) Letter to Niccolò Soderini, T 171, Vol 2, p.26.

BLESSED
JOHN HENRY NEWMAN
The Convert

CATHOLICISM
THE PIVOTAL PLAYERS
VOLUME I

Bl. John Henry Newman Study Guide written by Fr. Ian Ker

✠

BLESSED JOHN HENRY NEWMAN

The Convert

STUDY GUIDE WRITTEN BY

Fr. Ian Ker

Fr. Ian Ker is an English priest, scholar, and author. He is regarded as one of the world's leading authorities on Blessed John Henry Newman and his book, *John Henry Newman: A Biography* (Oxford University Press, 1988), is hailed by many as the definitive story of Newman's life. In addition to that biography, Ker has published more than twenty other books on Newman.

Fr. Ker teaches theology at Oxford University, where he is a Senior Research Fellow at Blackfriars, Oxford, and a member of the Faculty of Theology. He has taught both English literature and theology at universities in the UK and USA. He is also the author of *The Catholic Revival in English Literature* 1845-1961 (University of Notre Dame Press, 2003), *Mere Catholicism* (Emmaus Road Publishing, 2007), and *G.K. Chesterton: A Biography* (Oxford University Press, 2011).

BL. JOHN HENRY NEWMAN
The Convert
VIDEO OUTLINE — PART I

I. INTRODUCTION
   A. Key influencer of Vatican II
   B. Catholic thought in dialogue with the Enlightenment
   C. Lover of the truth
   D. Resisted liberalism

II. ANGLICAN LIFE AND TIMES
   A. Evangelical/Calvinist conversion at age 15
   B. Oxford as student, tutor, and fellow
   C. Exploring Anglicanism as a "middle way" between Catholicism
      and Protestantism
   D. Wrote *Idea of a University*
   E. Founded Oxford Movement in 1833 and wrote key tracts
      1. Dogma counter to Liberal view
      2. Sacramentalism of Anglican Church
      3. Anti-Catholicism (later recanted)
      4. Tract 90 (most famous): Challenged requirement to swear to
         39 articles of Anglican faith for professor and public officials.
         a. Regarded as a traitor to Britain
         b. Caused Newman to resign leadership of Oxford Movement
   F. Moved away from Oxford and spent time alone, reading the early
      Church Fathers and reflecting on prior viewpoint that Anglicanism
      is the right "middle way"

III. CATHOLIC LIFE AND TIMES
   A. Received into Catholic Church in October 1845
   B. Ordained a priest in 1847
   C. Rejected by Protestants and viewed with suspicion by Catholics
   D. Founded Birmingham Oratory

E. Rector of Catholic University in Dublin, which ended in his dismissal

F. Editor of *The Rambler*, lay-run publication that leaned to the left

G. In 1864, wrote spiritual autobiography *Apologia Pro Vita Sua*

H. Defending attack by Charles Kingsley

I. Wide, popular acclaim that restored Newman's reputation and silenced Catholic critics

J. Named a Cardinal by Pope Leo XIII in 1879

K. Died in 1890 and beatified by Pope Benedict XVI in September 2010

BLESSED JOHN HENRY NEWMAN

KEY INFLUENCER
of VATICAN II

John Henry Newman (1801-1890) was beatified in 2010 by Pope Benedict XVI. When he is eventually canonized, as he surely will be, he should also be declared a Doctor of the Church. Just as St. Robert Bellarmine was the Doctor *par excellence* of the Church of the Council of Trent, so Newman will be seen as his counterpart for the Church of the Second Vatican Council. It has become commonplace to call Newman "the Father of Vatican II," although there is only one text in the Council documents where his influence can be clearly felt. Nevertheless, he anticipated most of the other important documents, about which his writings offer illuminating commentary that is clarifying and also corrective where the meaning of Council documents has been distorted, exaggerated, or neglected.

Not only was Newman the towering theological figure behind the Council and the author of the seminal theological classic *On the Development of Christian Doctrine*, he was also one of the great prose writers of the nineteenth century, the author not only of a classic autobiography, the *Apologia Pro Vita Sua*, but also of such educational, philosophical, and spiritual classics as *The Idea of a University*, the *Grammar of Assent*, and the *Parochial and Plain Sermons*.

Newman's *Apologia Pro Vita Sua* traces his own religious and theological development. It was written in part to defend his integrity against the accusation of the popular novelist Charles Kingsley that Newman had been corrupted by his conversion to Roman Catholicism, an accusation that Newman knew was widely held. He wanted to show that the boy who had been brought up in what he later called "the national religion of England," consisting "not in rites or creeds, but mainly in having the

Bible read in Church, in the family, and in private," was the very same person as the Catholic priest, who had undergone considerable but authentic development, not corruption, in moving a long way from biblical Protestantism without abandoning or losing anything positive or authentic in his religious journey.

He was the same person as the teenager who underwent a conversion when the dogmas of Christianity became *real* rather than merely theoretical. Although he was influenced by an Evangelical schoolmaster, his conversion lacked the kind of emotional upheaval associated with Evangelical conversions. However, the Calvinist books his mentor lent him did influence him, as did, in a very different way, a history of the Church that contained long extracts from the Church Fathers.

Entering Trinity College, Oxford, at the exceptionally early age of 16, he gradually became more critical of the Calvinist theology he had embraced. But it was not until he became a fellow of Oriel College, where his views fell under the critical scrutiny of his theologically liberal colleagues, who emphasized the importance of reason in theology, that he finally abandoned Evangelicalism. However, the importance of personal conversion remained with him as did the reality of the fundamental Christian doctrines.

He was saved from theological liberalism by discovering the Fathers of the Church, whom he began reading systematically in 1828. However, he retained his sense of the importance of a critical theology, writing many years later as a Catholic: "Theology is the fundamental and regulating principle of the whole Church system." His study of the Church Fathers gained momentum in 1830 when he became a full-time research fellow, having been dismissed as a tutor at Oxford because of his attempted reform of the tutorial system.

He was influenced above all by the Greek Fathers, with their emphasis on the Incarnation, the Resurrection, the indwelling of the Holy Spirit, and the resulting divinization of the Christian. Newman was also influenced by their understanding of the Church as primarily the communion of those who have received the Holy Spirit through Baptism. When Newman finally accepted Catholicism as the fullness of Christianity, he brought all these positive influences with him into a Church where, among the laity, reading of the Scriptures and study of the Fathers was virtually unknown. Also at that time, an internally critical theology was hardly acceptable to a Church that felt itself already under siege from a hostile, modern, and increasingly secularized world.

In 1833, the new Whig (or Liberal) government brought before Parliament the Irish Church Reform Bill, which proposed suppression of ten Anglican dioceses in Ireland. The Oxford (or Tractarian) Movement effectively began in July 1833, due to the threat of state interference in the Church of England, including proposals to make doctrinal changes to create a comprehensive state church that would include all Protestant churches. In September, Newman published the first of his tracts for the *London Times*. It was these tracts, together with his sermons at St. Mary's, that were the principal means by which the Oxford Movement spread throughout the country. The central question facing the Movement concerned the nature of the Church: if it was not just a state church or the invisible evangelical church of true believers, then what was it?

To answer that question meant returning to the Fathers. Newman was the author of the two most important theological works of the Movement: *Lectures on the Prophetical Office of the Church* (1837) and *Lectures on Justification* (1838). These argued that the Church of England was a reformed branch of the Catholic Church and occupied a kind of *via media*, or middle way, between Catholicism and Protestant traditions.

However, in the summer of 1839, Newman began to have serious doubts about the Oxford Movement position. Rereading history, he was struck by how the pope at the Council of Chalcedon had upheld the orthodox Catholic faith against heretics, who divided into an extreme and a more moderate party. Then in September he read an article in which he was struck by a maxim of St. Augustine to the effect that there was no appeal against the universal Catholic Church. In 1841 he attempted in one of his tracts to argue that the "Thirty-Nine Articles" of the Church of England, which were assumed to establish its Protestant character, were susceptible to a Catholic interpretation, particularly as they had been formulated before the Council of Trent. Episcopal condemnations of the tract soon followed.

In 1842, Newman effectively left Oxford and moved to the village of Littlemore, where he began living in a religious community with some of his younger followers. However, in 1843, he returned to St. Mary's to preach the last of his university sermons—which were theological lectures rather than homilies—on the development of doctrine. He argued that the early Church had implicit knowledge of later doctrinal formulations. This view rested on defining faith as implicit rather than explicit reason, dependent on "antecedent probabilities or presumptions," which Newman had worked out in a series of sermons on faith and reason. Here is an excerpt from one of those sermons:

> "Reason, according to the simplest view of it, is the faculty of gaining knowledge without direct perception, or of ascertaining one thing by means of another. In this way it is able, from small beginnings, to create to itself a world of ideas, which do or do not correspond to the things themselves for which they stand, or are true or not, according as it is exercised soundly or otherwise. One fact may suffice for a whole theory; one principle may create and sustain a system; one minute token is a clue to a large discovery.

> The mind ranges to and fro, and spreads out, and advances forward with a quickness and a subtlety and versatility which baffle investigation. It passes on from point to point, gaining one by some indication; another on a probability; then availing itself of an association; then falling back on some received law; next seizing on testimony; then committing itself to some popular impression, or some inward instinct, or some obscure memory; and thus it makes progress not unlike a clamberer on a steep cliff, who, by quick eye, prompt hand, and firm foot, ascends how he knows not himself; by personal endowments and by practice, rather than by rule, leaving no track behind him, and unable to teach another. It is not too much to say that the stepping by which great geniuses scale the mountains of truth is

as unsafe and precarious to men in general, as the ascent of a skillful mountaineer up a literal crag. And such mainly is the way in which all men, gifted or not gifted, commonly reason—not by rule, but by an inward faculty.

Here, then, are two processes, distinct from each other—the original process of reasoning, and next, the process of investigating our reasonings. All men reason, for to reason is nothing more than to gain truth from former truth, without the intervention of sense; but all men do not reflect upon their own reasonings, but only in proportion to their abilities and attainments. In other words, all men have a reason, but not all men can give a reason. We may denote, then, these two exercises of mind as reasoning and arguing, or as unconscious and conscious reasoning, or as Implicit Reason and Explicit Reason. And to the latter belong the words, science, method, development, analysis, criticism, proof, system, principles, rules, laws, and others of a like nature.

Faith, then, though in all cases a reasonable process, is not necessarily founded on investigation, argument, or proof; these processes being but the explicit form which the reasoning takes in the case of particular minds. There is, first of all, an exercise of implicit reason, which is in its degree common to all men; for all men gain a certain impression, right or wrong, from what comes before them, for or against Christianity, for or against certain interpretations of Scripture, for or against certain doctrines. This impression, made upon their minds, is the object of science to analyze, verify, methodize, and exhibit. We believe certain things, on certain grounds, through certain informants; and the analysis of these three, the why, the how, and the what, seems pretty nearly to constitute the science of divinity."

–Excerpt from Newman's Sermon 13: *Implicit and Explicit Reason*

THE ORATORIAN MOVEMENT

When John Henry Newman was in Rome studying for the priesthood, he was intrigued by the Congregation of the Oratory of St. Philip Neri. Newman became an Oratorian priest and then went back to England and established the Oratory of St. Philip Neri at Maryvale, near Birmingham, in 1848. In his later years, Newman lived at the Birmingham Oratory, spending his time writing, preaching, and providing spiritual direction.

Founded in Italy by St. Philip Neri, the Oratory was a group of priests and lay brothers who lived in community without any formal vows, but bound by charity. The community began when Philip, recently ordained, met with a group of men in his room at the Church of San Girolamo. They focused on spiritual reading, discussion, and visiting churches, convents, and hospitals to tend to the sick and dying. Once the group became too large for Philip to manage on his own, he encouraged a few members to also become priests.

The community continued growing, and eventually acquired the church of Santa Maria in Vallicella in 1575. That same year, Pope Gregory XIII recognized the Congregation of the Oratory canonically. Oratory meetings gradually took on a more formal structure, called the "Exercises of the Oratory," which included mental and vocal prayer, comments on biblical readings, and the singing of hymns. New members did not go through a novitiate, as in a religious order, but lived within the community during their formation.

Today, there are more than 85 Oratories and 500 priests spread all over the world. Each Oratory is independent and self-governing, in a unique structure developed by St. Philip Neri, who wanted to avoid the centralized authority of a religious order.

QUESTIONS FOR UNDERSTANDING

1. John Henry Newman's knowledge of Scripture and his study of the writings of the early Church Fathers led him to accept Catholicism as the fullness of Christianity. How do Catholic teachings incorporate both Sacred Scripture and Sacred Tradition? (CCC 78-82, 104-05, 133-34, 141)

2. How did Newman define the Church, based on his reading of the Church Fathers? What does this say about the importance of Baptism? (Mark 16:15-16; Matt 28:19-20, CCC 977, 855, 1271)

3. Newman was intrigued by the Greek Fathers and their views on the Incarnation and the "divinization of the Christian." How is the "divinization of the Christian" to be understood? (John 17:3, 20-23; 2 Pet 1:3-4; 1 John 3:1-2; CCC 460)

4. What does "conversion" mean? Does it happen at one point in time or is it a continual process? Where do we see evidence of Newman's conversion during his life? (Acts 2:38, 2 Cor 5:17; Eph 4:20-24; CCC 1427-28)

5. The debate about faith and reason that Newman addressed again and again still continues today. Relying on Newman's insights, how would you explain that faith and reason are not just compatible but mutually supportive? Give examples of human reason in support of Christian faith. (CCC 154-156, 159)

QUESTIONS FOR APPLICATION

1. When have you experienced conversion in your own life? What's a personal example of when you consciously subverted your own will to better conform to God's will in your life?

2. Newman understood well both Catholic and Protestant positions. How can learning about his life and his teachings inspire us to work for greater ecumenism?

NOTES:

BL. JOHN HENRY NEWMAN
The Convert
VIDEO OUTLINE — PART II

I.   MAJOR WORKS

   A. *On Development of Christian Doctrine*

      1. Development, not deviations

      2. Doctrine as a "living organism"

      3. Need for "living authority" to avoid doctrinal corruption

      4. Embraced by theological liberals and conservatives

   B. *Idea of a University*

      1. Study of faith is an intellectual endeavor, appropriate for a university

      2. Religion/theology needs to be at the center of university courses due to its passion for the whole and the centrality of God

      3. Expulsion of religion from the university leads to constant succession of false pretenders to centrality

      4. Abstract knowledge is good in and of itself (i.e., the true "liberal" education)

      5. Universities are in the business of producing gentlemen and the Church is in the business of producing saints

   C. *Grammar of Assent*

      1. Relationship between faith and reason

      2. Assent, not certitude, more accurately describes the route to faith

         a. Notional assent: theoretical; abstract

         b. Real assent: concrete; tangible

      3. Real assent in faith best understood by reality of conscience

      4. Come to assent by weighing probabilities: use abstract arguments, hunches, instinct, memory, opinion of others, emotion, moral examples

II.   NEWMAN AS A "PIVOTAL PLAYER"
    A. Loved and sought to communicate the truth
    B. Saw modernity as a serious threat to Christianity and met the challenge with "thrilling dialogue" between the ancient Church and contemporary times

BLESSED JOHN HENRY NEWMAN

MAJOR WORKS

By the end of 1844, Newman was virtually certain that the Anglican Church was in schism, but he decided to test this growing conviction by developing his sermon on doctrinal development into a book, *An Essay on the Development of Christian Doctrine*. Not yet finished when Newman was received into the Roman Catholic Church on October 9, 1845, the book's thesis was that a living idea like Christianity has to develop in changing circumstances, not in order to be different but to remain the *same*.

After his conversion, Newman and his companions were offered the use of the former seminary building in Birmingham, which Newman renamed Maryvale. In September 1846, Newman left for Rome to begin a short course of study for the priesthood, where he encountered the Oratory of St. Philip Neri. To enable Newman and his companions to continue to live in community after their ordination in May 1847, they founded a new Oratory of St. Philip Neri in England at Maryvale, of which Newman was appointed superior.

In 1850 and 1851, Newman published two series of lectures, the first on *Certain Difficulties Felt by Anglicans in Submitting to the Catholic Church*, and the second on the *Present Position of Catholics in England*. The latter was his most brilliant work of satire, in which he attacked the English tradition of anti-popery.

In April 1851, Paul Cullen, then Archbishop of Armagh, visited Newman to ask for his advice on the founding of a proposed Catholic University of Ireland. In November, Newman was appointed president of the new university, and in the early summer of 1852, he delivered five of the *Discourses on the Scope and Nature of University Education*, which eventually became the first half of his treatise *The Idea of a University* (1873). In this celebrated educational classic, Newman defended the idea of a liberal education, by which he essentially meant the training of the whole mind, within a Catholic university. His skillful rhetoric did justice to the complexities of the Irish situation—a minority of bishops thought the idea of such a university totally impractical, the educated middle class thought it would just be a glorified seminary, and Irish nationalists disliked the idea of an English president—as well as to argue for the central place of theology among the branches of knowledge.

It was not until May 1854 that the Irish bishops formally confirmed Newman's appointment and the university's statutes. Newman wanted the new university to combine the Oxford college tutorial system with the continental professorial system, as at the Catholic University of Louvain, in Belgium, which was governed by the rector and the professors rather than the heads of colleges (as at Oxford).

In 1856, Newman published his second novel, *Callista*, which depicts the conversion of a post-pagan to Christianity (he clearly had in mind the typical secularized post-Christian of the late nineteenth century), in contrast to the conversion of an Anglican to Catholicism that he had portrayed in his first novel, *Loss and Gain* (1848). Interestingly, Newman does not deploy his famous argument from conscience for the existence of God, but rather the idea of St. Augustine's that our hearts are restless until they rest in God.

The same year also saw the opening of the university church on St. Stephen's Green in Dublin. A successful medical school was founded, as well as an academic journal, *The Atlantis*. But it proved extremely hard to find students because of the lack of secondary education for Catholics in Ireland, as well as the lack of support from England—not to mention that the government, which had recently founded the non-denominational Queen's Colleges, refused to recognize the university's degrees. But the chief reason for Newman's eventual resignation in 1858 was conflict with Cullen (by now Archbishop of Dublin), who understandably resented Newman's absences during vacations (he was still provost of the Birmingham Oratory). Cullen also refused to allow Newman to appoint his own vice-rector, and declined to approve a lay finance committee. Finally, he strongly disapproved of Newman's appointment of laymen, including leading Irish nationalists, to professorial chairs.

The question of the laity's role in the Church was now to loom large in Newman's life. In March 1859 he reluctantly agreed, as the one person acceptable to both sides, to temporarily take on the editorship of the liberal monthly *The Rambler*, which was threatened with Church censure. Newman disapproved of its critical attitude toward authority, while at the same appreciating the existence of a lay-run periodical that encouraged the intellectual life of all Catholics. He upheld the right of the laity to express their views on matters that concerned them, such as educational standards in Catholic schools.

After receiving a complaint from a seminary professor of theology, who disapproved in particular of Newman's observation that the laity had been consulted prior to the definition of the Immaculate Conception in 1854, he decided to resign, but not before publishing his famous article, "On Consulting the Faithful in Matters of Doctrine." Newman began the article by pointing out that he had used the word "consulting" in the sense in which a doctor consults the pulse of the patient, rather than that in which the patient consults the doctor. He also demonstrated (with examples) that the faithful were more steadfast than the bishops in upholding the doctrine of the divinity of Christ. It is important to note that Newman used the word "faithful" rather than "laity," as the "faithful" consists of priests, monks, and consecrated women in addition to lay people.

A Welsh bishop made an official complaint to Rome, and a list of the offending passages was sent to the Archbishop of Westminster, who unfortunately was ill and failed to forward them to Newman, whose silence convinced the Roman authorities of his disobedience.

THE GRAMMAR *of* ASSENT
Bishop Robert Barron

John Henry Cardinal Newman believed that *An Essay in Aid of the Grammar of Assent* was his most important work. Written in 1870 but of timeless importance, the *Grammar of Assent* addresses the process of coming to faith or belief in something, whether it's spiritual or not.

From the Enlightenment through today, many philosophers and thought leaders have questioned the existence of God and claimed that since you cannot prove the tenets of faith in a scientific way, they cannot be true. He called this approach "liberalism."

The obsession of modern thought throughout the 18th and 19th centuries was how to come to certitude. Newman believed that coming to certitude was not the process that mattered for belief, but that coming to assent was more relevant. He saw a big difference between the need to be certain and the quest to understand at a basic level, which is the basis of assent. We hardly ever get absolute certainty about most things, but we still have belief in many of them anyway.

Coming to assent involves much more than accepting an argument. Newman called the process the "illative sense"—the movement of the mind to the point of assent through formal conclusions, based on evidence, and then through informal conclusions based on many other things, such as peer group influence or "truths" passed down from others. We come to assent by an extremely subtle and unconscious process of weighing and accumulating "converging probabilities." For instance, my observations and what I've been told always lead me to believe something, even if it's not empirically certain.

There are two types of assent: notional and real. Notional assent deals in abstractions and propositions (the foundation of logical argument), while real assent deals with the particulars or the concrete. Real assent moves people to action in a way notional assent does not. For example, you might understand and agree with the logic in an argument, but still reject the conclusion because it is not real or tangible enough. In the movie *Juno*, a young woman seeking an abortion hears someone say, "Your baby has fingernails." The girl has heard all the logical arguments against abortion, but until she came face to face with this reality of fingernails, she could not make the decision to keep the baby. In other words, the fingernail comment led to "real" assent.

But how do we get real assent when it comes to believing in God? Newman explains that our conscience gives us concrete access to the reality of God. He calls conscience "a certain, keen sensibility, pleasant or painful, in virtue of which [we] call certain actions rights or wrong." Conscience is referred to as a "voice" and is oriented to something higher than ourselves. We are ashamed when we don't follow that voice. But since we can only be ashamed when in front of a person, there must be someone before whom we are responsible. And this is what Newman calls God.

In addition to these setbacks, Newman faced opposition to the Oratory School that he had founded to provide education for middle-class converts. A written attack by an Anglican clergyman, Charles Kingsley, in an 1863 magazine review proved to be a turning point. Newman's ensuing correspondence with Kingsley, published as a pamphlet, received a highly favorable review by a leading literary critic, R. H. Hutton, who wrote a scathing response to Kingsley's attack. Newman decided to take advantage of the publicity to write an explanation for his conversion, and turned the pamphlet into his autobiography, *Apologia Pro Vita Sua*.

In the book's last chapter, he undertook a general defense of Catholicism, particularly the infallibility of the Church, which was directed overtly at Protestants like Kingsley. But it was also aimed more covertly at extreme papalists, against whom Newman urged a balanced theology of authority and freedom in which the interaction, even conflict, of the Magisterium and theologians was depicted as creative and necessary for the Church's life. The book became a best seller and received almost universally favorable reviews.

For years now, Newman had been trying to work out a philosophy of faith in the face of growing secularization. In his *Oxford University Sermons*, he had argued that religious belief involved the same kind of informal reasoning that was unhesitatingly employed in other matters without accusations of irrationality. However, the problem still remained as to whether one could speak of attaining certitude in matters of religion, when the kind of certainty involved was so different from the objective certainty of logically necessary propositions and empirically verifiable factual statements.

At last, in 1866, he decided that he had been wrong to start with certitude rather than assent, and in 1870 the *Grammar of Assent* was finally published. In this book, Newman argued that where formal, logical inference or empirical demonstration is not possible, it is the accumulation of probabilities that leads to assent, and that this involves personal judgment, which Newman called the "illative sense," a sense that operates more or less unconsciously when the mind is deciding what to believe.

In 1867 Pope Pius IX announced that a General Council was to be held. Newman feared that the extreme papalists would press for a definition of papal infallibility, which he believed in but thought imprudent to publicly define. Newman refused three invitations to attend the Council as a theological consultant, including one from the pope himself. He thought that a council was uncalled for, as there was no heresy threatening papal authority, and dangerous, because there had not been sufficient preparation and study to justify such a sudden and unnecessary development.

In 1877, Newman added a lengthy preface to his Anglican *Lectures on the Prophetical Office of the Church*, in which he explained that the anomalies to be found in the history of the Church, such as superstition and abuse of power, were the result of the Church's difficulty in combining its three offices of teaching, worship, and government. Later that year, he was invited by his old college to become its first honorary fellow. Then, in 1879, the new Pope Leo XIII made him a cardinal, an honor that finally defeated suspicions of his orthodoxy.

Newman's health began to fail in the latter part of 1886, and he died on August 11, 1890. The pall over the coffin bore his motto: *Cor ad cor loquitur* ("heart speaks to heart"). On his memorial tablet in the Oratory were inscribed words he had chosen: *Ex umbris et imaginibus in veritatem* ("Out of the shadows and phantasms into the truth").

THE DEVELOPMENT *of* DOCTRINE
Bishop Robert Barron

When he was at mid-career and in the process of converting from Anglicanism to Roman Catholicism, Newman penned a masterpiece titled *On the Development of Christian Doctrine*. Newman argued that Christian doctrines are not given once for all and simply passed down unchanged from generation to generation. Rather, like seeds that unfold into plants or rivers that deepen and broaden over time, their various aspects and implications emerge in the course of lively rumination. It is assuredly not the case, for example, that the doctrine of the Trinity was delivered fully grown into the minds of the first disciples of Jesus and then passed on like a football across the ages. On the contrary, it took hundreds of years for the seed of that teaching to grow into the mighty tree of Augustine's formulations in the *De Trinitate* or Aquinas' complex treatise in the first part of the *Summa theologiae*. Newman concludes, "a real idea is equivalent to the sum total of its possible aspects." And those aspects appear only in the course of time and through the play of the lively minds that consider them. It is precisely in this context that Newman penned the most famous line of *On the Development of Christian Doctrine*: "In a higher world it is otherwise; but here below, to live is to change and to be perfect is to have changed often." Ideas change because they are living things.

Many, upon considering this view, will get nervous—as did many in Newman's day. Does this mean that doctrine is up for grabs? To get some clarity on this point, we need to delve a little further into Newman's great book and examine the criteria that he laid out to determine the difference between a legitimate development, which makes the doctrine in question more fully itself, and a corruption, which undermines the doctrine.

Newman presents seven criteria in total, but here we'll examine just three. The first is what he calls "preservation of type." A valid development preserves the essential form and structure of what came before. If that type is undermined, we are dealing with a corruption. Type can be maintained even through enormous superficial changes, as, to use Newman's own example, "a butterfly is a development of the caterpillar but not in any sense its image." By the same token, superficialities can remain largely unchanged even as the type utterly morphs, as happened, say, in the transition from the Roman Republic to the Roman Empire.

A second criterion is what Newman refers to as "conservative action upon its past." An evolution that reverses or contradicts what came before it is necessarily a corruption and not a development. In Newman's own words, an authentic development "is an addition that illustrates, not obscures; corroborates, not corrects the body of thought from which it proceeds." In accord with this idea, Christianity could be seen as the development of Judaism, since it preserves the essential teachings and practices of that faith, even as it moves beyond them.

A third criterion that Newman puts forward is what he calls "the power of assimilation." Just as a healthy organism takes in what it can from its environment, even as it resists what it must, so a sane and lively idea can take to itself what is best in the intellectual atmosphere, even as it throws off what is noxious. Both total accommodation to the culture and total resistance to it are usually signs of intellectual sickness.

QUESTIONS FOR UNDERSTANDING

1. Explain Newman's view regarding the development of Christian doctrine over time. How does the Church manage this development and decide what constitutes true and false development? (CCC 890-92, 2034)

2. In his book *The Idea of the University*, Newman concluded that universities were in the business of creating gentlemen, and the Church was in the business of creating saints. How does this relate to the universal call to holiness? How does the Catholic Church help its members to grow in holiness and become saints? (1 Pet 1:13-16; 2 Tim 1:9-10; CCC 2013-14, 2813)

3. In the *Grammar of Assent*, Newman developed his thesis that the key step to faith is *assent*, not *certitude*. Explain the difference between assent and certitude, as well as how they relate to belief in God.

4. What did Newman think was the most real or concrete evidence for the existence of God? (CCC 1706, 1776, 1778)

5. Newman suffered much in his life for speaking the truth. What is the core truth of Christianity, and how is sharing this truth the responsibility of all disciples? (John 1:1-5, 8:58, 14:6; CCC 638, 851)

QUESTIONS FOR APPLICATION

1. Do you embrace the universal call to holiness? How are you following the path to sanctity?

2. Newman was a deep thinker, and his intellect was instrumental to his conversion and profession of faith. How do you nurture the life of your mind with regard to the Catholic faith?

3. Have you ever stepped out of your comfort zone to speak the truth about Christ? What happened, and how did that affect you and/or the people around you?

G.K. CHESTERTON

The Evangelist

CATHOLICISM

THE PIVOTAL PLAYERS

VOLUME I

G.K. Chesterton Study Guide written by Dale Ahlquist

✠

G.K.CHESTERTON
The Evangelist

STUDY GUIDE WRITTEN BY
Dale Ahlquist

Dale Ahlquist is one of the most respected G.K. Chesterton scholars in the world. He is the president of the American Chesterton Society, which he helped found in 1996, and is the publisher of its magazine, *Gilbert.* He has written, edited, or contributed to more than fifteen books on Chesterton.

Ahlquist is also the host of the popular EWTN series, "The Apostle of Common Sense," and has given over 600 lectures on Chesterton all over the world, including at major universities, the Vatican Forum in Rome, and the House of Lords in London.

G.K. CHESTERTON
The Evangelist
VIDEO OUTLINE — PART I

I. INTRODUCTION

    A. Chesterton embodied the richness and capaciousness of Catholicism

    B. Love of paradox

    C. Believed Christianity would set right what was wrong with the world

    D. An evangelist because he fought back publicly against the critics of Christianity with articulate discourse and writing, proclaiming and celebrating the Gospel

II. LIFE AND TIMES

    A. Early Life

        1. Born in 1874 in London

        2. Baptized Anglican, but not brought up with a strong faith

        3. Interests centered on the arts, theater, drama

        4. Attended Slade School of Art in London

        5. Early life was nihilistic until he came to an attitude of gratefulness

        6. Started writing book reviews for a literary journal and discovered his true gift was writing

    B. Adult Life

        1. Married Frances Blogg in 1901; drawn deeper into Christianity; did not have children

        2. Wrote popular series of mystery fiction: *The Father Brown Stories*

        3. Intrigued by paradox and believed that the paradoxes of Christianity reflected the paradoxes of life

        4. Model of intellectual and religious discourse (could separate a person from his ideas)

        5. Lectured extensively in U.S. and elsewhere

        6. Became Catholic in 1922; believed "Catholicism is true [and] became a real messenger refusing to tamper with a real message"

        7. Took on the arguments of modernity against Catholicism

        8. Died at age 62 in 1936

III.   DISTRIBUTISM
    A. Chesterton's vision of Catholic social teaching
    B. Against Big Business, or the concentration of wealth among a few, and against Big Government that acted in place of the family; supported healthy and prosperous middle class.
    C. Believed that if community or individual had precedence over the family, society would disintegrate

G.K. CHESTERTON

INTRODUCTION

Gilbert Keith Chesterton was a physically large man with a very large intellect and imagination to match his appearance. Bishop Barron says that he "embodied the wealth and capaciousness of Catholicism" and was like "a fine champagne: intoxicating, sparkling, and rare."

The key to understanding him and his writing is to fully understand the notion of "paradox," or the coming together of seemingly contradictory things. Chesterton believed Christianity was full of paradoxes, yet was the only worldview that embodied the full truth of existence. Converting to Catholicism at age 48, Chesterton firmly believed that classic Christianity would set right what was wrong with the world.

Chesterton courageously answered the prevailing criticisms of Christianity with clarity and good humor. He cheerfully argued and defended the faith with skeptics and cynics, many of whom were his friends. However, he was always able to separate the person from his ideas, so could engage in positive religious discourse with anyone.

†

LIFE AND TIMES

G.K. Chesterton was born into a middle class family in the London suburb of Kensington in 1874. His parents surrounded him with love and encouraged him to pursue art and literature, but he was not raised in any creedal faith (his parents were Unitarian). Though he had a happy childhood, as a young man he followed a path of skepticism, agnosticism, and atheism that led him into a deep and suicidal depression. His deliverance came from clinging to "one thin thread of thanks" that not only saved him from self-destruction but set him on a new course, paved with wonder and joy, toward Christianity.

While his schoolboy friends all went off to Oxford and Cambridge, Chesterton enrolled in the Slade School of Art at the University of London, but soon dropped out, completely disillusioned with the decadence of modern art. He worked for a book publisher and soon pursued a career in journalism, and would make a living from his writing for the rest of his life. In 1901, he married Frances Blogg, but they were unable to have children. Frances played a key role in bringing Chesterton into Christianity, as he claimed she was the first Christian he had ever met who was happy.

Chesterton was a large man who made a large splash as a writer. When his articles began to appear in the newspapers, all of literary London wanted to know: "Who is G.K.C.?" His essays had a freshness and originality about them that combined verbal acrobatics with an overflowing joy and intellectual playfulness unsullied by the modern pessimistic spirit. The great literary figures of the time began to reach out to him: Max Beerbohm, H.G. Wells, George Bernard Shaw, and others. He became friends with all these people, but it was evident that he did not agree with them about much.

Chesterton was not afraid of controversy. On the contrary, he plunged into it. He defended tradition in the face of modernism, marriage in the craze of divorce, and belief in an age of doubt. While most of his readers thought he was merely striking a paradoxical pose, Chesterton surprised them when he admitted that he defended Christianity because he actually believed it to be true. The shock was intensified two decades later in 1922 when G.K. Chesterton was received into the Catholic Church. Ten years earlier, he had created a fictional detective, Father Brown, who happened to be a Catholic priest. Father Brown's success at solving mysterious cases was always surprising, as everyone dismissed him as being too innocent of the ways of the world. In addition, the Father Brown stories were little morality plays dressed up as murder mysteries. Just as a good mystery ends with an unexpected revelation, so Chesterton's own story jolted his audience when he entered the Catholic Church that, undetected, he had been writing about all along.

Chesterton's fame as a writer spread across the entire world. His works were widely translated, and he was invited to speak throughout Europe and North America. In every American city where he lectured, his visit was headline news and the talks were sold out. He had a reputation as a great writer, even though he could not be categorized. He was a journalist, a novelist, a poet, a playwright, a mystery writer, a social reformer, and a literary critic. He was also a Catholic apologist. After his conversion, he was especially sought after by Catholic institutions and events, which included being a visiting professor at the University of Notre Dame and a speaker at the International Eucharistic Congress in Dublin. Chesterton was even granted a private audience with Pope Pius XI, who made him a Knight of the Order of St. Gregory.

Amazingly, a few years after his death in 1936, Chesterton was almost forgotten. Recently his works have been enjoying a wide revival as they have been discovered by a new generation, and many of his neglected writings have found their way back into print.

He is not only being remembered, he is being celebrated as one of the great thinkers of the twentieth century. What might be seen as flaws in his character (his great size, his absent-mindedness) are things he transformed into opportunities for humor, and which served to make him more endearing. His laughter was always present in his writing, even when talking about very important things. He actually worked to dethrone the false god of seriousness, which many dour-faced Christians have made into a fearsome idol. He said, "The opposite of funny is not serious. The opposite of funny is not-funny." And even better, "It is a the test of a good religion whether you can joke about it."

He disarmed his opponents with charm and charity. He made friends out of enemies. In a world that ignores or even hates the Catholic Church, he made it attractive as a place of fullness and fulfillment and as welcoming as a warm hearth on a cold winter's night. He believed it is our true home on this earth, and is "larger on the inside than on the outside."

CHESTERTON'S DISTRIBUTISM

The term "Distributism" is as much misunderstood and misrepresented as the term "social justice." Social justice boils down to one thing: justice for the poor. Because of the inordinate gap between the rich and the poor, our society is out of balance. Catholic social teaching is the Church's attempt to address this injustice.

Distributism, often misunderstood, is Chesterton's application of Catholic social teaching. It is derived from Pope Leo XIII's encyclical *Rerum Novarum*, in which the pope says that justice must be "distributive," that is, available to all. Pope Leo maintains that industrial capitalism has reduced workers to a condition that is not much different than slavery. The wrong solution to this problem is the advocacy of socialism. The right solution, according to Chesterton, is that workers should become owners, enjoying the just fruits of their labor and not having to be utterly dependent on the whims of the rich or the welfare of the state. Only an enlargement of an independent middle class will reduce the huge gap between the rich and poor and make for a more balanced society. Chesterton and his friend Hilaire Belloc seized on this idea and became champions of social justice. For the greater part of his literary career, Chesterton devoted most of his energy to social justice, including editing his own newspaper, *G.K.'s Weekly*, for the last eleven years of his life. He opposed big government (whom he called "Hudge") and big business (whom he called "Gudge"), and he defended the common man in the middle.

Where Capitalism is concerned with the interests of the individual and Socialism is concerned with the interests of the community, Distributism is concerned with the interests of the family. Chesterton argued that Hudge and Gudge have attacked and separated our two most fundamental relationships: the love of a husband for his wife and the love of a mother for her child. He argues that the family is the basic unit of society. If the interests of the individual or of the community are given priority over those of the family, society will disintegrate. The system of wage-slavery separates father and mother from their children and from each other, as two incomes are increasingly necessary for survival. When the family falls apart, the State rushes in to fill the gap. This is seen in the form of mandated, state-sponsored education and legislation that defies natural law (i.e., that does not respect life). Chesterton is especially prophetic about modern culture and the ballooning of soulless education accompanied by the decline in morality and integrity in both politics and commerce. All these things are interconnected and Chesterton saw and explained the connection by saying, "Every political question is a religious question," and similarly, "Every economic issue is a moral issue." He aimed his blows equally at the political left and right, but the accuracy of his predictions is one of the reasons why the attempts to dismiss Distributism have not been successful.

A PERSONAL GLIMPSE

Fr. Vincent McNabb, a Dominican priest and a leader in the Distributist movement, was a great friend of Chesterton. Here are some of his impressions of the man:

A high activity of this humble soul was his unruffled patience. One incident may suffice. At the Eucharistic Congress in Dublin he sat beside a priest whilst a bishop gave an hour's address in Gaelic. At the end of the hour, during which he had been almost motionless, he heaved a smile and said, with a characteristic chuckle: "The finer points of that discourse escaped me." That smile and whimsicality were the fine, patient craftsmanship of humility.

It was hard to speak with Gilbert Chesterton and not to think—and think of God. Even the atheist who spoke with him, and who would have despised the God of Abraham, the God of Isaac, the God of Jacob, felt he would like to know about the God of Gilbert Chesterton—this God whom the very laughter of Gilbert Chesterton seemed to prove was such a lovably human, though transcendent being...

QUESTIONS FOR UNDERSTANDING

1. Chesterton said that his wife, Frances, was the first Christian he had ever met who was happy. What is happiness or joy? How are they related to faith? (CCC 384, 1718; 1 Pet 1:8-9; John 15:9-12; John 16:22; Ps 28:7, 33:21; Prov 16:20; Gal 5:22-23, CCC 1832)

2. Humility was one of Chesterton's notable attributes. What is it and why is it so important to the spiritual life? (Matt 18:1-4; 23:11-12; 5:3; CCC 2546, 2559)

3. How did gratitude lead Chesterton to become a Christian? What are key ways Catholics express gratitude to God? (CCC 1359-60,1418, 2097; 1 Thess 5:16-18)

4. What is a paradox? What are some paradoxes of Christianity? Explain the paradox of the Incarnation and of the Cross. (CCC 517, 525, 616-17)

5. How does Chesterton's Distributism align with Catholic social teaching? (CCC 1928-29, 1931-32, 1936-37, 1939-41, 2425-26)

QUESTIONS FOR APPLICATION

1. Gratitude was fundamental to Chesterton's ethic. List five things that you are grateful for right now. Keep a gratitude journal for thirty days, listing something new each day for which you are grateful.

2. Explaining the reason for his conversion, Chesterton said, "There are ten thousand reasons, all amounting to one reason: that Catholicism is true. It is the only thing that talks as if it were the truth; as if it were a real messenger, refusing to tamper with a real message." Do you agree with Chesterton? Why or why not?

THE DONKEY

This is one of Chesterton's most famous poems. The donkey, a paradoxical
creature, personifies the great Christian precept that the humble shall be exalted.

When fishes flew and forests walked
And figs grew upon thorn,
Some moment when the moon was blood
Then surely I was born.

With monstrous head and sickening cry
And ears like errant wings,
The devil's walking parody
On all four-footed things.

The tattered outlaw of the earth,
Of ancient crooked will;
Starve, scourge, deride me: I am dumb,
I keep my secret still.

Fools! For I also had my hour;
One far fierce hour and sweet:
There was a shout about my ears,
And palms before my feet.

NOTES:

G.K. CHESTERTON
The Evangelist
VIDEO OUTLINE — PART II

I.   ORTHODOXY
 A. Written as an explanation of how Chesterton came to believe in Christianity
 B. Argued that the tradition of Christianity is really startling and new
 C. Argued against any ideology that locks into a narrow and all-explaining system (e.g., scientific determinism, materialism, reductionism)
 D. Argued against religious skeptic David Hume and his views on the regularities of nature
 E. Discussion of Christianity's critics that the faith is filled with vices; however, different critics chose conflicting vices (e.g., fallen human nature vs. optimistic hope; timidity vs. courageousness)
 F. There are many paradoxes in Christianity
 G. Christianity is not a compromise but a radical and confident putting together of mutually exclusive extremes

II. THE EVERLASTING MAN
 A. Written three years after conversion to Catholicism
 B. Two parts:
  1. Argues against the evolutionist theory of H. G. Wells, that as man evolved from primitive to modern, he no longer needed religion and had the skills on his own to bring peace to the world
   a. Prehistoric cave paintings
  2. Argued against comparative religion theory, that all religions are the same and that Jesus is just one religious founder among many
   a. Jesus is the only religious leader who claimed to be God

III. WHY A PIVOTAL PLAYER?
 A. Against Puritanism, and filled with joy
 B. Against relativism, and argued fiercely about the uniqueness and truth of Jesus Christ and his Church

G.K. CHESTERTON

MAIN THEMES *in* CHESTERTON'S WRITINGS

Chesterton was immensely prolific and wrote about everything: current culture (including our own, which he seems to have foreseen), politics, war, sex, art, literature, science, technology, philosophy, psychology, morality, history, theology, and more. He is nothing if not quotable:

> *The Christian ideal has not been tried and found wanting. It has been found difficult and left untried.*

> *Men do not differ much about what things they will call evils; they differ enormously about what evils they will call excusable.*

> *To have a right to do a thing is not at all the same as to be right in doing it.*

> *The Bible tells us to love our neighbors, and also to love our enemies; probably because they are generally the same people.*

> *Angels can fly because they can take themselves lightly.*

There are three main themes that consistently occur in his writing. The first is itself a Trinitarian combination of wonder, joy, and thankfulness. Our only response to the gift of existence, of creation, of life, all of which we have done nothing to earn, is gratitude. For Chesterton, everything is informed by gratitude. "Thanks," he said, "is the highest form of thought." This naturally leads to a joy that always bubbles below the surface, no matter what miseries or sufferings float on top. Not only is everything a gift, but usually a surprise, as unexpected as it is undeserved. He would say that we should be thankful for the Christmas gifts we find in our stockings, but the best gift we can find in our stockings is our own two legs. And the only way to walk on these legs is with astonishment. For Chesterton,

---

the most astonishing thing about people is their lack of astonishment: "The world will never starve for want of wonders, but only for want of wonder."

The second main theme is freedom. Chesterton was always doing battle with any form of determinism or fatalism, whether it be scientific materialism or Calvinistic predestination. He believed that any assault on our free will is an assault on human dignity. Free will is one of the most sacred truths of Catholic theology, because it makes both our confession and our praise worthwhile. A man who does not believe in free will cannot even say, "please pass the mustard." Free will makes us responsible for our actions. Any political or economic system that manipulates or oppresses free will is evil. However there is a paradox: freedom is only truly enjoyed within rules. Chesterton said, "Catholic doctrine and discipline may be walls; but they are the walls of a playground." Or as Christ said, "The truth will make you free" (John 8:32).

This brings us to the third main theme, which is the ultimate focus of Chesterton's writing: God. He saw everything as pointing to God.

> You cannot evade the issue of God; whether you talk about pigs or the binomial theory, you are still talking about him. Now if Christianity be...a fragment of metaphysical nonsense invented by a few people, then, of course, defending it will simply mean talking that metaphysical nonsense over and over. But if Christianity should happen to be true, then defending it may mean talking about anything or everything. Things can be irrelevant to the proposition that Christianity is false, but nothing can be irrelevant to the proposition that Christianity is true.

ORTHODOXY

Although all Chesterton's books and essays profoundly and provocatively point to the truth, there are two books that must be considered essential: *Orthodoxy* and *The Everlasting Man*. Both books are about the convergence of truth, how everything points to the same thing—in this case, Christianity: "A man is not really convinced of a philosophic theory when he finds that something proves it. He is only really convinced when he finds that everything proves it."

The key to understanding *Orthodoxy*—and to understanding Chesterton—is becoming familiar with the concept of paradox. In *Orthodoxy*, Chesterton constantly makes statements that seem contradictory or run counter to our expectations. However, there is a scriptural precedent for paradox: the first shall be last and the last shall be first; the humble shall be exalted; blessed are the poor; a virgin shall give birth; the dead shall rise. These are all familiar, biblical paradoxes. However, when Chesterton tells us that the madman is not the man who has lost his reason, but the man who has lost everything *except* his reason, we are surprised. Likewise, we are surprised that Chesterton found his way to Christianity not by studying the defenses of it, but rather the attacks on it. He saw that most modern philosophies lead not only to madness but to self-destructive madness, as they get stuck on one idea that may seem reasonable, but is inadequate to explain the whole truth of things.

Paradox also includes the idea of two truths that appear to contradict each other and yet are both true. Chesterton used the example of courage, which is "a strong willingness to live accompanied by a readiness to die." In other words, he that lays down his life will gain it (Luke 17:33). Truth is a balancing act of apparently contradictory ideas, and the only thing that has maintained that balance throughout history is the Church as the Body of Christ. The Church is built on the ultimate paradox of Jesus Christ, who is fully God and fully man. He is not half one and half the other. He is not a thing different from either, but both at once. Plus, the salvation that comes through Christ's suffering and death on the Cross is indeed another sign of paradoxical contradiction.

THE EVERLASTING MAN

If *Orthodoxy* is the story of how Chesterton made his way to Christianity, *The Everlasting Man* is about the place where he arrived. This is the book that helped bring C.S. Lewis to the Christian faith. Chesterton's approach to history, art, poetry, philosophy, and theology is brilliantly concise and unique, even though he takes on Eden, Babylon, Egypt, Israel, Greece, Rome, Carthage, Buddha, Mohammed, and Christ. All history and philosophy and religion converge on a single point, in Bethlehem. Everything that has happened since then can only be explained by the truthfulness of the claim that Christ made about himself: he is God in the flesh. Other explanations fail to explain.

Chesterton argues that man is naturally monotheistic, but is always tempted away from God, and then finds himself separated from God. ("The most ignorant of humanity know by the very look of earth that they have forgotten heaven.") The subsequent search for God is also natural to man, and accounts for most of the development in art and culture throughout the world. But as the search falters, two things happen: the poetic attempts to explain the supernatural (mythology) give way first to the purely natural (reason and philosophy), and then to the unnatural (perversion and demon worship). The merely materialist approach (reason alone) does not satisfy man's spiritual needs, and without the truth, man will attempt to satisfy those needs with evil spirits. (We often forget that Christ arrived in a land plagued by demonic possession.) Only God himself can satisfy the needs of our mind and spirit. Theology and philosophy, faith and reason, came together for the first time in Christianity.

Everything about Jesus' life was unique and paradoxical. His teachings were not typical of his time, and would be a challenge in any age. To say that they were not well received would be an understatement. He was put to death. But the story did not end there. He came back to life. But neither did the story end there. He founded and continues to live in the Church.

The people of that Church have a message for the world. That Church has a spotted but fascinating history. It has often appeared to be defeated or destroyed. But that Church has always come back to life, "for it has a God who knew his way out of the grave."

✝

THE LEGACY *of* G.K. CHESTERTON

Why is Chesterton a Pivotal Player? He was a journalist who not only defended the Catholic faith in the most secular of settings, but also defended common sense, which is nothing other than natural law. He turned modern philosophy on its ear. In a world that becomes more unhinged every day, his criticisms have never been refuted—only ignored. His writings force us to ask fundamental questions, which are answered satisfactorily only by Christianity.

Chesterton is a model of lay spirituality and of Christian joy. He defended the family as well as a social philosophy that is consistent with his theology. His goodness flowed from his words, which still today bring people into the Church. Though he was physically huge, the hugest thing about him was his humility. Yet he was not afraid to take a stand against the world, and said, "The world is always converted by the saint who contradicts it most."

ORTHODOXY, CHAPTER 4,
"The Ethics of Elfland"

This elementary wonder, however, is not a mere fancy derived from the fairy tales; on the contrary, all the fire of the fairy tales is derived from this [wonder]. Just as we all like love tales because there is an instinct of sex, we all like astonishing tales because they touch the nerve of the ancient instinct of astonishment.

This is proved by the fact that when we are very young children we do not need fairy tales: we only need tales. Mere life is interesting enough. A child of seven is excited by being told that Tommy opened a door and saw a dragon. But a child of three is excited by being told that Tommy opened a door. Boys like romantic tales; but babies like realistic tales—because they find them romantic. In fact, a baby is about the only person, I should think, to whom a modern realistic novel could be read without boring him.

This proves that even nursery tales only echo an almost pre-natal leap of interest and amazement. These tales say that apples were golden only to refresh the forgotten moment when we found that they were green. They make rivers run with wine only to make us remember, for one wild moment, that they run with water.

I have said that this is wholly reasonable and even agnostic. And, indeed, on this point I am all for the higher agnosticism; its better name is Ignorance. We have all read in scientific books, and, indeed, in all romances, the story of the man who has forgotten his name. This man walks about the streets and can see and appreciate everything; only he cannot remember who he is. Well, every man is that man in the story. Every man has forgotten who he is. One may understand the cosmos, but never the ego; the self more distant than any star. Thou shalt love the Lord thy God; but thou shalt not know thyself. We are all under the same mental calamity; we have all forgotten our names. We have all forgotten what we really are.

All that we call common sense and rationality and practicality and positivism only means that for certain dead levels of our life we forget that we have forgotten. All that we call spirit and art and ecstasy only means that for one awful instant we remember that we forget.

QUESTIONS FOR UNDERSTANDING

1. What are the three main themes in Chesterton's writing? How can
    you use these themes to evangelize? (CCC 905, 2044, 2472; CCC 257,
    1730)

2. What is free will and how is it perfected? (CCC 1730-33, 1738)

3. Why is Jesus Christ not "just one religious leader among many"? (John 8:58; 14:6-10; Col 2:9; CCC 469, 653)

4. How did Chesterton show that he was a committed disciple of Jesus Christ and a model of lay spirituality in the contemporary world? (CCC 899-900, 1832)

QUESTIONS FOR APPLICATION

1. Choose one of Chesterton's quotations and write about how it illuminates a Christian truth.

2. How do you exhibit your discipleship? How are you a "model of lay spirituality"?

NOTES:

MICHELANGELO

The Artist

CATHOLICISM

THE PIVOTAL PLAYERS

VOLUME I

Michelangelo Study Guide written by Dr. Anthony M. Esolen

✠

MICHELANGELO
The Artist

STUDY GUIDE WRITTEN BY
Dr. Anthony M. Esolen

Dr. Anthony Esolen is a professor of English at Providence College and translator of classic works. He has written for publications such as *The Claremont Review of Books*, *Magnificat*, *First Things*, *The Catholic Thing*, and *Touchstone Magazine*, of which he is a senior editor. He has translated Dante's *Divine Comedy*, Lucretius' *On the Nature of Things*, and Torquato Tasso's *Jerusalem Delivered* into modern English.

Esolen graduated *summa cum laude* from Princeton University in 1981. He pursued graduate work at the University of North Carolina, receiving his M.A. in 1981 and his Ph.D. in 1987 in Renaissance Literature. In addition to Providence College, he has taught at the University of North Carolina and Furman University. Esolen studies languages and reads several, including Italian, Latin, Anglo-Saxon, German, and Welsh.

MICHELANGELO
The Artist
VIDEO OUTLINE — PART I

I. INTRODUCTION
    A. Eighth-century dispute over the use of icons/spiritual depictions
    B. St. John of Damascus made Catholic tradition of visual art possible
    C. Draw through the physical image to the transcendent reality it represents

II. LIFE AND TIMES
    A. Born in Caprese in 1475 and raised in Florence (family of stonecutters)
    B. Apprentice to Ghirlandaio; learned the fresco technique
    C. Lived in palace of Lorenzo de' Medici among intellectuals and worked in sculpture garden
    D. Lorenzo dies and Medici family loses power; influence of Dominican Fra Savonarola rises
    E. Went to Rome in 1496, completes the *Pietà*
    F. Returned to Florence in 1501, completes the *David*
    G. Back to Rome in 1505, commissioned to sculpt Julius II's tomb (never completed)
    H. Completed Sistine Chapel ceiling, 1508-1512
    I. Completed *The Last Judgment*, 1535
    J. Chief architect of the new St. Peter's Basilica, 1546
    K. Died in 1564

III. THE PIETÀ
    A. *Mary*
        1. Serene and youthful although age 45-50
        2. "Virgin Mother, the daughter of your Son"
        3. New Eve: forever young Mother of the Church
        4. Ark of the Covenant

B. *Pietà*

  1. Designed as an altar piece; connected to the sacrifice of the Mass

  2. Mary offers her crucified Son as a gift of life (Eucharist)

IV. THE DAVID

 A. Renaissance humanism: beauty and glory of the human being

 B. Foreshadowing of Christ

  1. Son of David and the new Adam

  2. Archetype of the human according to God's intention

MICHELANGELO

MAN FULLY ALIVE

Bishop Barron begins his commentary on Michelangelo by referring to the brave witness of Saint John Damascene (John of Damascus), the monk who opposed attempts by the Byzantine emperor Leo to obliterate images of God the Father and God the Son from Christian churches. That's a brilliant way to begin. It reveals how much is at stake: a right view of man's relationship to God; a right view of the humanity of Christ; and the very possibility for the greatest achievements in the visual arts that the world has known. In an earthly sense, John of Damascus made Michelangelo possible, but it was the Christian faith that made John of Damascus possible.

Let's look at this a little more closely. Leo was not moved by hatred of the faith, as are the image-smashers of our time. He was moved by a mistaken piety, prompted by the new players on the world's stage, the Muslims. Recall that Muslims are strict iconoclasts. When the Muslims in 1453 finally wiped the Byzantine Empire from the face of the earth, they wiped out a great deal of art too. They turned the Hagia Sophia, the Church of the Holy Wisdom, into a mosque, and plastered over mosaics and frescoes depicting scenes from the life of Jesus, saints in glory, and the Son of God as ruler of the universe.

The Muslims then said what poorly educated secular people in our day say: Christians conceive of God as a being like ourselves, only greater. That gets things exactly backwards. Our faith teaches us not that God is built like a man, as is mythical Zeus or Apollo, but that man is made *in the image of God.* Hence the Jews were prohibited from making graven images, lest they reduce God to their small imaginings and collapse back into the paganism and idolatry of their neighbors.

But what does it mean to be made in the image of God? We could speculate on that for the rest of our lives. Does it mean that we possess reason?

That we are free, unlike the beasts? That we long for wisdom? That we are oriented toward what is beyond us—that God himself is our rising sun? Yes, it means all that, but fortunately we needn't be philosophers to enter the discussion. "I praise you, Father, maker of heaven and earth, and give you thanks," said Jesus, "that you have hidden these things from the wise of the world, and revealed them to the childlike" (Matt 11:25). Jesus is the icon of the invisible God, as Bishop Barron reminds us, quoting Saint Paul (Col 1:15). "Show us the Father," said the apostle Philip, having spent three years in the company of Jesus, yet not understanding his divine identity. "Philip," said Jesus out of his infinite patience, "whoever sees me sees the Father" (John 14:8-9). So it's as Bishop Barron says: Christian portrayals of Christ are a continuation of the life on earth, in the flesh, of the Word of God. Jesus has blessed the body forever by uniting it with his divinity.

Now you might conclude that this viewpoint is simply a permission slip for Christian artists that says: "You may go ahead and paint and sculpt just as the pagans did." But that would be a colossal error. Christian art has attained a depth of insight into what man truly is, which even the humanistic sculptors of ancient Greece could never conceive. We may say that the revelation of Christ is the *pivot* upon which the history of art has turned, not from this thing to that thing, but from truth in two dimensions to truth in the infinite measure of the Word made flesh.

To see why, I'd like you to consider three famous sculptures. One is of the pagan god Apollo in the Vatican Museum, the *Apollo Belvedere*. Michelangelo saw this sculpture and knew that it was long esteemed as the greatest work from the ancient world. Apollo is a

Apollo Belvedere, Vatican Museum, Rome. MARIE-LAN NGUYEN / WIKIMEDIA COMMONS

The Thinker, Musée Rodin, Paris. VALDORIA / WIKIMEDIA COMMONS

young man with curly hair, a clear brow, smooth cheeks, and, to my eye, a vacant look on his face. No surprise, that vacancy. For those Greek gods forgot their momentary sorrows. They were interested in human affairs; they liked justice well enough; they were pleased by sacrifices and songs; but they dwelt on Olympus, and ate ambrosia, and whatever sorrows they felt for the moment they could forget as easily as we might flick away a tear.

Now go to Paris, to the garden of the *Musée Rodin*. Here we see the second most readily recognizable sculpture in the world. It is Rodin's *The Thinker* (1904). Gone is the fresh face of the god of music. The figure is rugged, his muscles are taut, and he is leaning forward in intense concentration. What is he thinking about? Whatever it is, it's not ambrosia. We might say that Apollo is a god in idealized human form, but we would never say that about *The Thinker*. He is man searching with his mind; a man searching for truth. God has made him to be so. The Greek sculpture is of an *anthropomorphic god*; Rodin's sculpture is of *theomorphic man*.

Now at last we turn to the best-known sculpture in the world, Michelangelo's *David*. Michelangelo has learned everything that the ancient sculptors had to teach him. And, without Michelangelo, Rodin's work would be inconceivable. Bishop Barron asks us to look at the athleticism of the young man, standing without a stitch of clothing and without any armor, for God alone is his sword and shield. Look now at David's face and compare it with the face of Apollo. We are in a different universe, as Rodin, centuries later, well understood.

David, Galleria dell'Accademia, Florence. WORD ON FIRE

David's brow is furrowed and tense. He glares at Goliath. His eyes are wide open. His look is not one of foolish contempt. David is not a swaggerer. There is in that look a mingling of fear, resolve, anticipation, hatred of the wicked, and prayer for the strength of God. No Greek sculptor ever conceived such a thing. "Christ reveals man to himself," said the council fathers at Vatican II. They might have been looking upon *David* when they said so. St. Irenaeus said that the "glory of God is man fully alive," and that is what Michelangelo presents to us.

✝

LIFE AND TIMES

Moving to the artist's life and times, let's reflect on another feature of the *David*: the right hand that holds the stone that will kill Goliath.

Whenever I show my students that hand, they fall silent—they are stunned. That hand could never be mistaken for the hand of child. It is large, heavy-boned, and muscular. A prominent vein runs from the thumb to the wrist. Look at the finger joints and the knuckles. Do you see that they are swollen? Those are the calluses of hard physical labor.

The young David kept sheep for his father, Jesse. I don't know whether shepherding covers your hands in calluses, but the grueling work of quarrymen, stonecutters, masons, and sculptors—Michelangelo's work—surely does.

So we have in this sculpture the mind that sees and the hands that make. But how can the mind see well or the hands be deft without an education?

As a boy, Michelangelo learned how to paint frescoes when he

David, Galleria dell'Accademia, Florence. WORD ON FIRE

worked in the studio of Domenico Ghirlandaio, one of the most-sought artists in Italy. Of course, the pupil eventually far, far surpassed the teacher, but we should consider what the pupil was doing and learning.

He was learning how to *make* paints—you couldn't go to the hobby store to buy things ready-made. You had to get your hands dirty in the very stuff. You had to grind the minerals in a mortar. You had to know what would happen to the colors after they dried or aged. You had to know how to apply plaster to a wall. You had to know how long the wet plaster could absorb the paint. You had to know how much of the wall to cover at one time. You had to know how to draw up an enormous *cartone*, a "cartoon," to guide you in your placement of the figures on so large a space. You had to know how to draw. You had to know how to work with others, some of them boys like yourself, others young men almost ready to venture forth on their own, and still others the old masters of the studio, all of them busy at the same time on the same wall.

To work with a team of boys and men covering a wall in the Church of Santa Maria Novella in Florence was akin to working with a similar team cutting high-quality blocks of marble from the quarries of Settignano, where Michelangelo spent much time in his youth. It's impossible to put a precise value on these and similar experiences, which were the norm for artists of that time and were indispensable for the breathtaking achievements of the Renaissance. There was not then, as now, an unnatural and counterproductive division between the work of the mind and the work of the hands. That division has resulted in a great deal of "philosophy" divorced from human realities, and the disappearance from popular arts of hard-won craftsmanship and the knowledge distilled from centuries of tradition.

We can look at Michelangelo's education from the other direction too, going from the hand to the mind. When Michelangelo got a little older, Ghirlandaio sent him and a couple of the other boys to the villa of the *de facto* ruler of Florence, Lorenzo de' Medici. Lorenzo had gathered around him a group of illustrious scholars and artists. They didn't give courses to paying students. That wasn't the idea. They conversed with one another, and executed works of art or scholarship in the ambience of their conversations. Imagine it. You're an intelligent, ardent young man, and suddenly you find yourself in the midst of men brimming over with ideas—philosophers, publishers, artists, theologians, and historians. They spend their days working and talking, and you are brought into their midst.

We can glimpse a little of what this meant if we go to one of Ghirlandaio's frescoes in the Tornabuoni Chapel of Santa Maria Novella, *The Annunciation of the Angel to Zachariah.*

The Annunciation of the Angel to Zachariah, Tornabuoni Chapel of Santa Maria Novella, Florence. PUBLIC DOMAIN

We see in the painting not a Jewish synagogue but a magnificent Catholic church from Ghirlandaio's time, with people in Italian Renaissance garb. If you look at the group of four men in the foreground to the left, you'll see a few of the people whom the young Michelangelo got to know at Lorenzo's academy: Marsilio Ficino, the Platonist philosopher; Cristoforo Landino, the humanist scholar and editor; Angelo Poliziano, the poet; and Demetrius of Chalcedon, one of the Greek scholars who came to live in Italy after the Muslims had made life in Greece intolerable.

The cynical way to interpret this—the wrong way, as I see it—is to say that Renaissance pride in oneself and one's country had overtaken the sacred. That's not how Michelangelo interpreted it. What we have here, really, are the ages in conversation. The annunciation of the birth of John the Baptist cannot be, for the Christian, something that happened a long time ago and is now over. Return to the lesson that John of Damascus hammered home. When we say Emmanuel, God-with-us, we don't just mean that God is a divine companion of mankind as he saunters down the ages. God is himself the Creator of time and the sustainer of life at every moment. Isn't that also what the Eucharist teaches us? When did Christ sacrifice himself for us? Two thousand years ago upon Calvary, and eternally upon all the altars of the world. If we understand this, we see that events in the history of salvation cannot pass away. They are with us still, and *we are with them*.

✝

HOLY MOTHER CHURCH

Some people may now say that it was a historical accident that the Church was the patroness of great art back then, and that it need not have been so. We can do without the Church, they claim, and still have another Michelangelo arise among us.

I'll express my reply as precisely and delicately as possible. "No, we can't."

We may have a lot of good art now, although in reality I believe that all Western arts have suffered an astonishing collapse. Entire *kinds of art* have disappeared. But I think that a dispassionate observer of human history will have to admit the fact that the greatest human art, whether the painting of Caravaggio, the sculpture of Michelangelo, the poetry of Virgil and Dante, the drama of Aeschylus and Shakespeare, or the music of Bach and Beethoven, is inconceivable without the religious impulse. Art is both our play and our offering to God. Holy Mother Church is not accidentally but naturally the mother of arts, as she was the mother of Michelangelo.

Return to Bishop Barron's wonderful discussion of Michelangelo's *Pietà*, in which the Lord, taken down from the Cross, lies in death upon the lap of Mary. Michelangelo was deeply indebted to Dante—and which Italian artist was not? At the climax of Dante's *Paradiso*, St. Bernard offers a prayer to Mary that she pray to God for Dante, so that the poet will behold the ultimate Truth, the beatific vision of God. It is the vision that man as human desires, and also the vision that man as artist desires. There is none greater.

Pietà, St. Peter's Basilica, Vatican City. PUBLIC DOMAIN

Now then, Bernard's first words are these: *Virgine Madre, figlia del tuo Figlio (Virgin Mother, daughter of your Son).* Mary is "younger than sin," as the novelist Léon Bloy put it. Hence the woman who holds Christ upon her lap is young, eternally young. Artists had portrayed her otherwise; see the fainting Mary to the left of the Cross in Andrea Mantegna's tour-de-force *Crucifixion.* But this Mary is not only young; she is timeless. The chances and changes of this world have not etched a mark upon her countenance. But her face is still utterly different from the vacant, boyish face of the *Apollo Belvedere.* "Mary remembered all of these things," says St. Luke, "and treasured them in her heart." One thing remembered was old Simeon's prophecy that a sword would pierce her heart, and we see that memory on her face in the *Pietà.*

Mary is not outside of suffering like an Olympian goddess. She is right in the middle of it. She is through it and in it and with it because she is with her Son. That look upon her face is *pietosa:* more than we pity Mary, she pities us; she is the mother of mercy. Mary enthroned is the Church herself, our Mother, bringing Christ to us. Hence her left hand extended, as if to give Jesus to the world, and her right hand pressing him close, but through the veil of her garment, just as the priest shows Christ to us when he lifts the monstrance holding the Blessed Sacrament.

St. Bernard had advised Dante that to attain the end of his spiritual journey, he should gaze with devotion upon Mary. Michelangelo recalls the remarkable words Bernard uses: Dante is to look into the face that most resembles Christ. Here a theologian might stumble at what a child will understand at once. Why does Mary most resemble Christ? She is his mother. Think of that. It is far more elemental than, "Mary was kindest to the poor" or "Mary was most ardent in her prayer life." Mary is his mother. Michelangelo showed the visual connection. So his Mary might have been the younger and beloved sister of Jesus. Study their youthful faces. Account for the young man's beard and his squarer jaw and heavier cheekbones. Tuck his hair under the veil. Now look at Mary and see that mysterious look of knowledge, patience, gentleness, serious thought, and complete love. Do you not see Jesus there?

But the Church is also our Mother, as Mary is the Mother of the Church. She brings Christ to us by her preaching, certainly, but also bodily in the Sacrament of the altar. Mary too, in Michelangelo's sculpture, is bringing Christ to us, welcoming us to behold him and to unite ourselves with them in their familial love.

So now we understand why Michelangelo's Mary, if she stood up, would be eight feet tall. It isn't just a solution to a practical artistic problem. Here, Mary is the throne of Jesus. He is naked and she is clothed, but you can see the prominence of her breasts beneath her robe: "Blessed is the womb that bore you," cried the woman in the crowd to Jesus, "and the breasts that nursed you!" The baby Jesus, the all-powerful Word made speechless and helpless, used to lay in the lap of his mother and take life from her breasts. The man Jesus, the ever-living God made subject to death, lies in the lap of his mother—and brings us life. We are meant to be with Jesus both at his birth and at his death, sustained by our mother Mary and the holy Church.

An artist of Michelangelo's stature comes once in a thousand years, but not at all to people who have forgotten who they are. The Church reminds us that we are children of God as part of her role on earth as *Mater et Magistra*—Mother and Teacher.

THE FOUNDATIONAL INFLUENCE *of* LORENZO DE' MEDICI *and* SAVONAROLA

In Florence while still in his teens, Michelangelo witnessed the beginnings of the Italian Renaissance, fostered by the *de facto* leader of Florence, Lorenzo de' Medici, and stymied by the Dominican friar, Girolamo Savonarola.

Lorenzo took Michelangelo into his home and allowed him to study and work in his sculpture garden. In a turbulent time in Italian politics, Lorenzo had brought peace to Florence and was loved and trusted by his people. According to Michelangelo's biographer, Bruno Nardini:

> Lorenzo distributed no alms, but of the painters he ordered pictures and frescoes, of the architects he demanded projects for palaces, fortresses and gardens, of the sculptors he asked statues for public squares and fountains for courtyards. To the scholars he proposed translations and comments on the classics, opening his precious library to them. In his home the most brilliant engineers of the time were welcomed like brothers. With philosophers he, himself a philosopher, discoursed on man, God, and the ultimate meaning of life. Lorenzo was truly the center and guiding spirit of that great movement known as "Florentine humanism," which was soon to blossom into the Italian Renaissance.

At the same time, Fra Savonarola, the Prior of San Marco Monastery, preached against the vanity and sinfulness of secular art and new ideas. He believed nothing was worthwhile unless it led us to Christ and communicated the many truths of the Gospel. Lorenzo greatly respected his honesty and faith, even though Savonarola preached against much of what Lorenzo was fostering. On his deathbed at age 43, Lorenzo called for Savonarola to give him last rites, saying: "I have never found a real friar but him."

Savonarola preached to large crowds in Florence against homosexuality, adultery, public drunkenness, immodest dress, and other moral transgressions. He led a "bonfire of the vanities" where things that he believed could lead to sin were burned in the public square. Objects burned often related to vanity, such as mirrors, cosmetics, and fine dresses. Other targets were playing cards, musical instruments, and books and artwork believed to be immoral. Savonarola also criticized the Curia and practices of the church in Rome, which drew the ire of Pope Alexander VI, who excommunicated him in 1497. In spite of all his political and prideful posturing, however, he did write a few acclaimed Christian treatises, most notably *The Triumph of the Cross.*

Michelangelo stayed three years in Lorenzo's palace, hearing Savonarola preach and rage from the pulpit and in the streets. Both men contributed greatly to his formation as an artist and as a Christian. Nardini explains that Michelangelo "listened, read, questioned and nourished his soul at that font of knowledge that was to make of him the great conciliator between the classic and the modern world, between the pagan and the Christian message."

QUESTIONS FOR UNDERSTANDING

1. Explain the ban on making images of God that started with the Hebrews. How has the Incarnation affected this perspective? How do holy images, Michelangelo's and others, propagate the faith? (Exod 20:4-5; Deut 4:15-19; Col 1:15; CCC 2129-2132)

2. What is the Catholic view of the body? How does Michelangelo's *David* showcase this view? (CCC 364, 369; 1 Cor 15: 42-49; Rom 8:22-23; CCC 991, 997-999; Mt 25:31-46)

3. Explain how King David relates to and foreshadows Jesus in Scripture. How did Michelangelo's *David* represent this foreshadowing? (I Sam 17:41-51; 2 Sam 7:1-16; 1 Chron 22:6-10; Matt 1:1; Heb 1:5-9)

4. What does the *Pietà* communicate about Mary and Jesus in terms of their relationship? What is communicated about the Eucharist? (CCC 964, 1391)

5. How is the Church our *Mater et Magistra (Mother and Teacher)?* (Eph 5:25-28, 32; Rev 21:9-11; CCC 507, 2040, 2047; Matt 28:18-20, 1 Tim 3:15, 1 Cor 2:12-13; CCC 2032-34, 2037-38)

QUESTIONS FOR APPLICATION

1. How has beauty been a route of access to God for you? Please give some examples.

2. What is your personal view of how body and soul relate? When, if ever, have you prioritized the material at the expense of the spiritual? When, if ever, have you prioritized the spiritual at the expense of the material?

3. How are you a mother and teacher of the faith?

NOTES:

MICHELANGELO
The Artist
VIDEO OUTLINE — PART II

I. THE SISTINE CHAPEL

A. History

    1. Completed in 1481, papal chapel and site of conclave to elect pope

    2. Built to mirror Solomon's Temple

    3. Team of artists commissioned to paint walls

B. Ceiling

    1. Nine scenes from opening of Genesis with prophets, sibyls, and Christ's ancestors also depicted

    2. First triad: The Creation of the World

        a. Separation of light from darkness

        b. Creation of sun and moon, often representing Jesus and Mary

        c. Creation of sea creatures

    3. Second triad: The Creation and Fall of Human Beings

        a. Creation of Adam: energy of God flowing from finger to finger

        b. Creation of Eve: material and spiritual coming together

        c. Fall and expulsion from the Garden of Eden

    4. Third triad: The Story of Noah and the Effects of Sin

        a. Fleeing the great flood; ark in background as a church

        b. Sacrifice of Noah as priest

        c. Drunken and naked Noah being discovered by his sons

C. *The Last Judgement*

    1. Jesus centered as the sun with humanity revolving around him

    2. Judging all: the saved above and damned below

II. WHY IS MICHELANGELO A PIVOTAL PLAYER?

A. Proves that the artistic and beautiful can be a vehicle to the spiritual

B. Confirms the key principle of the Incarnation: "God became human so humans could become God." The divinization of humanity is the greatest humanism possible.

MICHELANGELO

THE SISTINE CHAPEL

St. Augustine often cited a verse from the Book of Wisdom: "Thou hast ordered all things in measure, number, and weight" (11:20). That verse is a touchstone for medieval and Renaissance art, music, and poetry. Bishop Barron's reading of the principal sections of the Sistine ceiling suggests what it implies. The artists strove to embody those principles of universal harmony in their works. There's nothing accidental or insignificant in the work of God, whether we're talking about the physical universe at any one moment, or its history through time, or the workings of grace in the history of man. Not a sparrow falls to the earth without the will of the Father. Every hair of our heads is numbered. Therefore if man's art is to reflect the art of God, it too must be made "in measure, number, and weight."

Raphael's School of Athens, Apostolic Palace, Vatican City. PUBLIC DOMAIN

Dante wrote his *Divine Comedy* in 100 cantos, not 97. Shakespeare never inserted a comic moment into his tragedies just for dramatic effect: the drunken porter in *Macbeth* who answers the door in the wee hours of the morning has one of the most significant speeches in the play. If you look at Raphael's celebrated *School of Athens*, you are meant to relate the posture of Plato and Aristotle to the books they carry: the elder Plato points toward heaven as he carries the *Timaeus*, his dialogue about the order of creation, while Aristotle is gesturing forwards and earthwards to the world of man as he carries his *Ethics*. Above them and between them in the sky is the vanishing point of all the lines of perspective. It's also the center of an arch above the two philosophers. That arch was not to be found in ancient Athens. It's the arch of Saint Peter's as it's being rebuilt. Plato and Aristotle are, so to speak, *almost* in the Church. Or perhaps they *are* in the Church. Not one detail is accidental or the product of a whim.

So when we look upon the work of Michelangelo, we must keep that order in mind. We must also keep in mind, as discussed in Part I, that the events of salvation history are with us still, and *we are with them*.

Michelangelo's most famous painting, *The Creation of Adam*, is prominent on the ceiling of the Sistine Chapel. What has he painted? It is an event that happened long ago, true. But it is also an event happening now: God the Creator makes man in his image. That space between the finger of God and the finger of Adam is the greatest "painting" of nothing in all the history of art. How narrow it is! As Bishop Barron suggests, you can almost feel the pulse of God's energy about to bring man to life. Yet it *is* a space, and might as well be an abyss, because it marks the difference in *being* between the Creator and the creature. That space, as well as the grand and beautiful form of Adam, expresses the great truth in Scripture: "In the image of God he made him" (Gen 1:27).

How long did it take for that painting to come into being? Michelangelo spent many months at that one piece, on his back on the scaffolding that towered like lacework up in the dizzying heights. However, his hands by then had known years upon years of instruction in quarries, studios, and churches. And his heart, mind, and soul had been formed by more than twenty centuries of pagan, Jewish, and Christian thought. For truth, wherever it is to be found, belongs to the Church.

Consider Michelangelo's painting of the Fall of Man, also grounded in the truth of our sinfulness. Bishop Barron notes that the forbidden fruit comes from a fig, not an apple tree. Figs symbolized the sexual organs in the Old Testament, and the rest of Genesis after the Fall is a saga of misadventures in sexual relations and family life. Look at the posture of Adam. It is shameless ambition in action. He has to grab hold of one branch while extending his arm to the farthest point to grab the fig from the half-serpent, half-human figure of Satan. His genitals are almost in Eve's face. She is almost competing with him as her knees bump against his shins, while she twists herself upwards and backwards to reach for the fruit over her head. Between them and the fig tree, and starkly visible against the sky, is what surely looks like a dead thing—a tree of death in Eden or perhaps the Tree of Life, now bare. It is a jagged stump, foreshadowing the Cross of Christ.

Look then at Adam and Eve as they are expelled from Eden. They are awkward and even ugly, as Bishop Barron suggests. Adam seems to be stepping upon Eve's foot. His hair is tangled and spiky, as of a demon thrust from heaven. Where is the grandeur of Adam as at the moment when God breathed into him and he became a living soul? Where is the sweet and open-eyed beauty of Eve? Paradise lost.

Then, looking at Michelangelo's scenes from the life of Noah, Bishop Barron reminds us of the connection that Christian theologians and artists have long drawn between the Church and the ark of Noah (1 Peter 3:20), and the womb of Mary and the Ark of the Covenant (Rev 11:19-12:1-2). For the Ark of the Covenant contained three precious things: the tablets of the Ten Commandments, the rod of Aaron, and manna from the desert. That was the Old Covenant, in sum. Mary will hold in her womb the New Covenant, not a collection of things but Jesus. He is the New Law; he is the new High Priest; and he is himself the bread from heaven. If you want to survive the storms of this life of sin, you need to get into the Ark, which is the Church. That's why we often see Noah and his ark on baptismal fonts.

Let's move on to the painting of Jonah, which stands above the altar and the *Last Judgment* (painted later). There's a whale with a flailing Jonah and the resurrection of the dead—why? Of all the prophets, why should Jonah be so closely associated with the resurrection of the dead to damnation or to glory?

MICHELANGELO: *The Artist*

It requires a sort of reading that is now unfamiliar. It's not like reading a news article or a novel that proceeds from one event in someone's life to another, as if we were walking down a road. It's like the kind of listening that polyphonic music demands: you hear two or three independent melodies sung simultaneously, each reflecting upon the other. But once you get the hang of it, it's like opening a door from the black and white of Kansas to the brilliant color of Oz, a world endlessly rich in meaning.

Look at the *Last Judgment* and see Mary, huddling beneath the right arm of Jesus. Wasn't Michelangelo thinking of the Eve he had painted before on the ceiling above? Eve, not yet made in the flesh but existing in the mind of God, huddles beneath the *left* arm of the Father. Why? Look at the color of Jesus' hair. Isn't it the same as the color of Adam's hair as he is driven out of Eden? Why? Look at the famous gesture of the lone man who is being pulled down to hell, his hand covering one of his eyes. How is it like and unlike the gesture of Eve in shame? Why the eyes? Why one eye? We never come to the end of such art. Only a vision of God's universal order and significance found in Christianity can sustain it.

Around Christ, the Judge, we see a throng of saints who are being raised to glory. Each brings something to witness to his devotion or his martyrdom. St. Sebastian is the beautiful youth on the far right, making a motion as if to shoot an arrow. St. Peter is near to Christ, holding the keys to the kingdom. Now look at the bald saint just below Christ's feet. In his right hand he holds a knife. In the other, he holds a sagging skin. It is St. Bartholomew the apostle, who, according to tradition, was flayed alive. So that is his own skin he is holding.

Except that it is not his skin. Michelangelo has painted Bartholomew as a bald man with a beard. The skin is of a clean-shaven man, with hair—close-cropped, curly black hair—and a prominent nose, broken in a fight when he was a youth. Michelangelo has painted himself into the *Last Judgment* as the limp and horrible skin. Recall the words of St. Paul, who tells us in the Letter to the Romans what it is to be a fallen man. It is to see the good and want it, but to do what is evil anyway. It is to be divided in your own members. "Wretched man that I am!"

cries the apostle. "Who shall deliver me from this body of death?" (Rom 7:24).

Look at Adam, as God imparts to him the spark of life. Look at David, ready to take on Goliath. Now look at that skin; look at Michelangelo's self-portrait. The same artist, the greatest who ever lived, brings us Adam and David and *that*—moved by the same truths about man when he created all of it. If you understand that, you understand the mind of the Renaissance.

A TRUE HUMANIST

Michelangelo is one of a handful of Italian artists whom speakers of English—Protestants, most of them—loved so well, they called them by their first names alone: Michelangelo, Raphael, Sebastian (del Piombo), Guido (Reni), Titian, and a few others. Secular professors of art still do. Yet we cannot really understand their work outside of the revelation of Christ. As Bishop Barron suggests in his conclusion, Michelangelo was not a humanist despite his Catholic faith, but *because* of it.

Michelangelo shows us that there can be no true humanism without God because man was made by God, for God, and in his image. To pretend otherwise is to try to live in a world that does not exist. It is to be that fellow in the painting of the Flood, the one whom Bishop Barron says resembles a pagan river god. He's drinking and consoling himself while he can, perhaps with fantasies that help him forget, while the waters of death keep rising.

The loss of that faith in the artistic world means a loss of vision into human nature and human beauty. C. S. Lewis said it well. Strive for heaven, and you get earth in the bargain. Strive for earth only, and you lose both.

When we hear the word humanist now, we think of someone who believes in man rather than God. That sort of humanism, to adapt the words of Flannery O'Connor, is a step away from the gas chamber. The twentieth century is evidence of what happens when man thinks he can do without God.

Now, when we talk about a "Renaissance humanist" such as Michelangelo, we mean in the first place something straightforward and very important. A humanist is someone given to the *studia humanitatis*, the "studies of humanity." Erasmus, who published an authoritative edition of the Greek New Testament, was a humanist. The Dominican friar Savonarola, who studied the early Church Fathers, was a humanist. If you learned classical Latin and Greek and you read Homer and Virgil, you were a humanist. You could be a saint like Thomas More or a cynic like Machiavelli; a painter of sacred art like Botticelli or a composer of bawdy prose like Rabelais—all humanists. It implied nothing philosophical or theological. It was in that sense like being a carpenter or a tailor—someone who has pursued a line of work or a course of study.

There was, I'll admit, a little more to it than that. There was a special focus on man that distinguishes the art of the Renaissance from the art of the Middle Ages; though we should take care not to exaggerate the difference. Giotto, supposedly a "Renaissance" artist, was born in the thirteenth century and was a contemporary of Dante, and both men were in their graves long before Chaucer wrote *The Canterbury Tales*. But let us grant that special focus. It still does not mean that you are going to believe that man is glorious. The humanist Machiavelli believed that man was selfish and treacherous. The humanist theologian John Calvin taught that fallen men were utterly depraved. In Renaissance art, we see extremes of optimism and pessimism that are foreign to the high Middle Ages. The Renaissance person who on Monday sings of the glory of man will on Friday bemoan his shame and disgrace. Nor do you have to change your mind to do that. All you have to do is to move from one side of a Renaissance room to the other.

QUESTIONS FOR UNDERSTANDING

1. Not much is known about Michelangelo's interior life. What can we learn about his faith based on his works? (Matt 7:15-20; CCC 901, 1704)

2. Explain what Bishop Barron means when he said that creation was an "act of division and God continues to separate." (Gen 1:1-10, 2:21-23; Lev 20:26; Luke 11:23, 12:51-53; Matt 25:31-43)

3. In the center panel of the Sistine Chapel ceiling, what truth about the creation of man is represented by God's pointing finger? (Gen 2:7; CCC 33, 362, 366)

4. Explain how Noah's ark represents the Church (Gen 6:11-14, 7:1; 1 Pet 3:18-22; CCC 845, 1180).

5. Explain how Mary represents the Ark of the New Covenant. How does Jesus embody the three things that were carried in the original Ark of the Covenant? (Exod 25:8-16; Rev 11:19-12:1-2; CCC 2676; Heb 9:3-4; Mt 5:17-19; John 6:48-51; 1 Chron 23:13; Heb 5:1-6)

6. Michelangelo placed his Jonah depiction in the Sistine Chapel right above *The Last Judgment*. Why could Jonah be so closely associated with the resurrection of the dead? (Jon 2:1, 11 and 3:1-5; Matt 12:38-42)

7. How is Christianity the "greatest humanism possible," as Bishop
    Barron states? (CCC 460, 461, 463)

QUESTIONS FOR APPLICATION

1. How do your outward works show your faith to others? In what
    ways could you make them more expressive and definitive of your
    beliefs?

2. Select a favorite religious work of art. Spend ten minutes in silent meditation using this work as your focal point. What insights did you gain by this meditation?

3. What works of art are in your parish church? What do they signify? Choose one work of art in your church that you are unfamiliar with and do some research to find out more about its background and what it represents.

ANSWER KEY

CATHOLICISM
THE PIVOTAL PLAYERS
VOLUME I

Facilitator Guide written by Peggy Pandaleon

CATHOLICISM
THE PIVOTAL PLAYERS
Answer Key

ST. FRANCIS *of* ASSISI
The Reformer
QUESTIONS *for* UNDERSTANDING, PART I

1. **What moved Francis to embrace the leper, which was an act most repugnant to his nature? (Matt 16:24-25; 2 Cor 5:15-20; Rom 14:7-8; Gal 2:20)**

    Answer: Francis did not go to the lepers spontaneously, by his own will, or because he was moved by human and religious compassion. "The Lord," he writes, "led me among them." Francis came to the poor after his conversion out of love for Christ.

    The profound motive for his conversion was not social but evangelical. Jesus had formulated the law once and for all in the Gospel:

    > If anyone wishes to come after me, he must deny himself, take up his cross and follow me. For whoever wishes to save his life will lose it; but whoever loses his life for my sake will find it. (Luke 9:23-24)

    Francis' conversion was not about choosing between wealth and poverty, nor between the rich and the poor, nor between belonging to one class or another. It was about choosing between himself and God, between saving his life and losing it for the Gospel.

2. **After his conversion, Francis dedicated himself to the corporal and spiritual works of mercy. What are those? Why are they important? (CCC 2447; Matt 25:31-46; James 2:14-17; 1 John 3:11, 16-18)**

    Answer: The corporal works of mercy tend to the needs of the body and include feeding the hungry, sheltering the homeless, clothing the naked, visiting the sick and imprisoned, and burying the dead.

    The spiritual works of mercy tend to the needs of the spirit and include instructing, advising, consoling, comforting, forgiving, and bearing wrongs patiently.

    These works of mercy are important because they are the outward signs of faith in Christ and the loving response to his commandments, especially to "Love one another as I have loved you."

3. **How was the lifestyle of St. Francis and his Friars Minor similar to the lifestyle of the early Christian community? (Acts 2:42-47; 4:32-35; Luke 9:1-3)**

Answer: Both communities had a total trust in God's providence. They prayed, ate, and celebrated the Eucharist together. They shared all that they had and did not keep material possessions for themselves, but lived in common. People joined the early Christian community and St. Francis and St. Clare's orders in great numbers. Francis followed Jesus' actions literally when he sent his brothers out to preach the message of the Kingdom of God and to take nothing for the journey.

4. **Where did Francis' joy come from? How did it affect his evangelization? (1 Pet 1:8-9; Rom 15:13; CCC 736, 1832, 1829)**

Answer: Francis' joy came from being deeply in love with Christ and being filled with the Holy Spirit. Joy is one of the fruits of the Holy Spirit, evident in those who are filled with his grace. Joy is also a fruit of charity, along with peace and mercy. Francis' entire life was filled with charity and mercy, especially to the poor and suffering.

Francis abandoned himself totally to God and to his purposes with absolute trust in the Lord, so he had no reason to be troubled. He was able to preach the Gospel and bring others to Christ without fear or worry because he firmly believed that God would provide all he needed. This deep faith gave him true freedom and the power to accomplish his mission on earth.

ST. FRANCIS *of* ASSISI
The Reformer
QUESTIONS *for* UNDERSTANDING, PART II

1. How did Francis "restore the 'flesh and blood' to the mysteries of Christianity"? Why was that particularly important at that time in Church history?

   Answer: During Francis' time, there was much corruption in the Church and the people were hungry for reform. Many Christian teachings had become theoretical and conceptual, and did not translate into the way people lived their lives. Francis literally lived the way Jesus did, and created a large following who did the same, proving that indeed the Christian life could be lived literally, and lead to joy and peace, as Christ promised.

   One small example of making the mystery of the Incarnation more tangible was Francis' establishment of the Christmas nativity scene, complete with live animals and songs of glory and praise.

2. In the video, Bishop Barron talks about two graces that Francis prayed for about a year before he died. What did he pray for and how did God answer his prayer?

   Answer: Francis prayed that he would feel the pain of Christ's passion and that he would love Christ with the same love that made Christ sacrifice himself for us.

   We know God answered his first request, as Francis received the stigmata shortly thereafter. We have no sure way of knowing the type of love for Christ that was in his heart; however, we have evidence that Francis loved his fellow man, especially the poor and suffering, with a Christlike love. As Francis is a saint, it seems very certain that these two requests were granted by the Lord.

3. St. Francis embraced suffering with great joy, even seeming to seek it out. Why do you think he did that? How is suffering related to penance? (Rom 8:16-17; Col 1:24; CCC 977, 1494, 1434-35, 1032)

   Answer: Bishop Barron attributes Francis' embrace of suffering to his desire to be fully united with Christ in all things, to "take up his cross" and become like Christ. As adopted children of God in Christ through baptism, we are all meant to share in his suffering and death, as well as in his eternal life and glory.

   In his apostolic letter *Salvifici doloris* ("redemptive suffering"), St. John Paul II explains:

Down through the centuries and generations it has been seen that in suffering there is concealed a particular power that draws a person interiorly close to Christ, a special grace. To this grace many saints, such as St. Francis of Assisi, owe their profound conversion. A result of such a conversion is not only that the individual discovers the salvific meaning of suffering, but above all that he becomes a completely new person. He discovers a new dimension, as it were, of his entire life and vocation. This discovery is a particular confirmation of the spiritual greatness which in man surpasses the body in a way that is completely beyond compare.

Penance is a type of reparation for sin. While Christ's death merited forgiveness of sins and eternal redemption for all who believe in him, there is still need for temporal reparation for the effects of sin. St. Paul says that by our own suffering and sacrifices, we can make up for what is lacking in the "body of Christ that is the Church." So we can offer our own suffering as penance for other members of the Body of Christ, including those who have died and are in purgatory.

Saint John Paul II goes on in the same encyclical mentioned above to explain:

> Christ has accomplished the world's Redemption through his own suffering. At the same time, this Redemption lives on and in its own special way develops in the history of man. It lives and develops as the body of Christ, the Church, and in this dimension every human suffering, by reason of the loving union with Christ, completes the suffering of Christ. It completes that suffering just as the Church completes the redemptive work of Christ.

4. **In what way would you describe St. Francis as a "reformer" during his lifetime? How do you believe the reform took shape after his death from the seeds he had planted? (CCC 1430-32; Ps 51:12; Rom 12:2)**

    Answer: Francis reformed the Church through his radical conversion and his example of Christian holiness.

    First and foremost, Francis reformed himself by repenting of his pride and materialism, subjugating his ego to God's will, and surrendering his whole life to the providence of God. He lived publicly in radical detachment from the goods of this world and chose singular attachment to the purposes of God.

    By the example of his and his brothers' lifestyle, which embraced poverty, simplicity, purity, and obedience, he showed all Christians what it truly means to follow Christ. He redefined authority away from power and toward service. Church leaders could not ignore the sheer number and commitment of his followers. Through service to the poor and suffering, Francis put into action Christ's command to "love one another."

    The Church bears many fruits of the seeds of Francis' life. Some examples include: priority of serving the poor and protecting the innocent; reforms to improve the purity and simplicity of clerical life; many religious orders that follow a similar rule; and sensitivity to our responsibility to care for all of God's creatures.

ST. THOMAS AQUINAS
The Theologian
QUESTIONS *for* UNDERSTANDING, PART I

1. **In what two ways was Thomas a radical of his time? How can being a Christian today also be seen as radical by the culture? (John 15:18-19; Matt 8:21-27; James 4:1-10; 1 Pet 4:1-4)**

   Answer: Bishop Barron describes Thomas as a double radical due to his interest in Aristotle and his Dominican affiliation. Aristotle was denounced and thought to be off-limits to Christians because he was a pagan philosopher. The Dominican Order was in its infancy then, and many were appalled at the radical lifestyle demanded through its vows. Dominicans were committed to poverty as mendicants, who had to beg or receive charity for all their needs. Most considered a mendicant lifestyle shameful in the thirteenth century.

   The ways of Christ are not the ways of the world, so a true, practicing Christian will often be seen as a radical due to beliefs and practices that are different from the culture. Jesus said that the world would hate his disciples just as the world hated him (John 15:18-19). To be faithful, Christians are called to seek out the will of God and follow it, even if it is counter-cultural. Western culture's obsession with wealth, pleasure, power, and honor cannot be shared by a true disciple of Jesus. The Christian's view on the sanctity of life, marriage, and religious freedom will often be radically different than the average American's.

2. **What or who is God, according to Christian belief? What does Thomas add to our understanding of God? (Exod 3:14; Isa 40:18; Ps 139:1-18; CCC 213, 230-31, 279, 290, 338)**

   Answer: We believe that God is the Creator, sustainer, and sanctifier of all that exists. He is eternal, unchangeable, immaterial, and infinite, and he remains a mystery, for as St. Augustine said, "If you understood him, it would not be God."

   Thomas brought additional insight to the Christian doctrine of God by explaining how God is not one being among many or even the Supreme Being. He is being itself, or, as Thomas said, "*ipsum esse subsistens*"—the "sheer act of 'to be' itself" through which all things come into existence. God is the answer to the question, "Why is there something instead of nothing?"

3. **The Church professes, and Thomas teaches, "God is one." What does this mean? (Deut 6:4; Isa 44:6; CCC 212-213, 228, 234-37)**

   Answer: The statement "God is one" has layers of meaning. First and foremost, it means that the God of the Israelites is the one, true, and only God—no other gods exist. This is the foundation of the whole Mosaic Law, and was professed in a prayer called the *Shema*: "Hear O Israel! The Lord is our God, the Lord alone."

"God is one" also means that God exists in perfect unity within the Trinity of divine relationships: Father, Son, Holy Spirit. "God has left traces of his Trinitarian being in his work of creation and in his Revelation throughout the Old Testament. But his inmost Being as Holy Trinity is a mystery that is inaccessible to reason alone or even to Israel's faith before the Incarnation of God's Son and the sending of the holy Spirit" (CCC 237).

Also, God is the same yesterday, today, and tomorrow, and he is unchangeable and eternal, so seen as "one."

4. **How is Jesus Christ the fullest revelation of God on earth? (John 1:1-3, 18; Eph 1:15-21; CCC 151, 516, 561, 648)**

   Answer: Jesus always existed as the second Person of the Trinity, the Son of God with a divine nature. Through the Incarnation, Jesus became fully man without losing his divinity, so now he is one person with two natures. He lived among us and showed us by his words and deeds the most complete revelation of God the fulfillment of the revelation that was begun at creation. John says in the first chapter of his Gospel: "No one has ever seen God. The only Son, God, who is at the Father's side, has revealed him."

   Christ's resurrection confirms his divinity and all the claims he made while on earth. "The Father's power 'raised up' Christ his Son and by doing so perfectly introduced his Son's humanity, including his body, into the Trinity. Jesus is conclusively revealed as 'Son of God in power according to the Spirit of holiness by his resurrection from the dead'" (CCC 648)

ST. THOMAS AQUINAS
The Theologian
QUESTIONS *for* UNDERSTANDING, PART II

1. How did Thomas answer those who believed that faith and reason are incompatible? (CCC 154-159, 286)

   Answer: Thomas explained that faith and reason are not incompatible because they come from the same source—God. Our creator has given us minds that reason along with grace, so that we can come to know him, love him, and serve him: "Believing is an act of the intellect assenting to the divine truth by command of the will moved by God through grace" (CCC 155).

   God has revealed many things that conform to our reason and validate the Christian faith. Creation itself testifies to the existence of a Creator whose existence is not contingent on anything else.

2. Describe what the soul is and how it relates to the human body. How should we treat the body based on this understanding? (Gen 2:7; Eccles 12:7; CCC 33, 362-366, 382)

   Answer: The soul and the body are unified, and thus our human nature is both physical and spiritual. God created the human body from the dust of the earth and then he breathed life into it (Gen 2:7). This breath of God is our soul. The body dies and decays, yet the soul is immortal. At the resurrection on the last day, our souls will be reunited with our bodies and we will live, body and soul, eternally with God.

   Thomas said the soul "forms" the body, meaning that it is not contained by the body but contains the body and gives it life. The soul is everywhere in the body, just as God is everywhere in the universe.

   We should treat our bodies with reverence and respect as the handiwork of God: "It is a human body precisely because it is animated by a spiritual soul, and it is the whole human person that is intended to become, in the body of Christ, a temple of the Spirit. Man may not despise his bodily life. Rather he is obliged to regard his body as good and to hold it in honor since God has created it and will raise it up on the last day" (CCC 364).

3. What does it mean to be "made in the image and likeness of God"? How has sin changed that and what restores it? (Gen 1:26; CCC 356-57; Rom 3:23; CCC 2809, 705, 1701-02)

   Answer: "God said, 'Let us make man in our image, after our likeness.'" Being made in God's image is not physical, but has to do more with the mind and the will, according to Thomas.

Humankind has an infinite capacity of mind and will, which orders us to something beyond our human nature. We are not satisfied by any truth, but want Truth itself. We are not happy with any good, but want Good itself. This desire for God comes from being made in his image and likeness.

St. Paul said, "All have sinned and fallen short of the glory of God." We retain the image of God but have lost his likeness (or his glory) due to sin. The Incarnation restores man to a full likeness with God, as Jesus combines the human and divine natures in one person. Both natures are united in Christ, so that through faith in him, our sins are forgiven and we are restored to the likeness (or glory) of God: "It is in Christ, Redeemer and Savior, that the divine image, disfigured in man by the first sin, has been restored to its original beauty and ennobled by the grace of God" (CCC 1701).

4. **In Thomas' view, humans are in great need of the incarnate Word. Who is the incarnate Word and why do we need him? (John 1:1-4; CCC 241-42; Acts 4:10-12; John 14:6-7; Matt 1:21; CCC 1741)**

    Answer: Jesus Christ is the incarnate Word, existing prior to the beginning of time as the second Person of the Trinity. We need him because only Jesus, through his suffering and death, restores us to friendship with God. Jesus "saves us from our sins." His death paid the price for our sins and opened heaven again to humankind, who had been barred from eternal life with God due to original sin. Jesus even said himself, "I am the way, the truth, and the life. No one comes to the Father except through me."

ST. CATHERINE *of* SIENA
The Mystic
QUESTIONS *for* UNDERSTANDING, PART I

1. **What evidence do we have that God loved us first, and loves us unconditionally?** (CCC 270, 315, 545; Ps 145:8-19; John 3:16-17; Luke 15:3-7)

   Answer: "In the creation of the world and of man, God gave the first witness and universal witness to his almighty love" (CCC 315). In all eras, God has been faithful to his people, as he is our Father, providing for our needs and answering our prayers.

   Even after man sinned and turned away from God, he showed his mercy by sending forgiveness through his only Son, Jesus Christ, who died for the forgiveness of sins. This sacrifice is the "supreme proof of his love" (CCC 545). God's mercy endures forever, and he will never refuse a repentant sinner. This is illustrated by the parable Jesus told of the shepherd who looks for one lost sheep out of his flock of a hundred. The shepherd represents God, who will go to great lengths to bring back each and every sinner.

2. **How should we love God?** (Deut 6:4-7; Matt 22:37-40; John 13:34; CCC 1822-23, 1878, 2093; 1 John 4:19-21)

   Answer: Jesus said, "Love the Lord your God with all your heart, with all your soul, and with all your mind. This is the greatest and the first commandment. The second is like it: Love your neighbor as yourself" (Matt 22:37). Jesus ratchets up this language later, when he tells us to "love one another as I have loved you" (John 13:34). Jesus' love is total and unconditional, which now becomes the model of how we are to love others.

   Jesus makes charity/love the greatest commandment and unites love of God with love of neighbor. Loving God cannot be separated from loving one another. As Saint John wrote: "If anyone says, 'I love God,' but hates his brother, he is a liar; for whoever does not love a brother whom he has seen cannot love God whom he has not see" (1 John 4:20).

3. **In what ways did St. Catherine follow the commandment to "love one another" during her life on earth? What are the characteristics of this type of love?** (CCC 1825, 2443-44, 2447; 1 Cor 13:4-7)

   Answer: After a period of years in a reclusive state, Christ called St. Catherine out of her parents' home to minister to the poor and forgotten in her community. She worked as a nurse and supported prisoners, even those condemned to death. She worked tirelessly performing the corporal works of mercy.

The Lord also asked her to perform the spiritual works of mercy, bringing people closer to himself and to his cross. She exhibited great courage and love in traveling to Avignon to convince the pope to return to Rome.

In his first letter to the Corinthians, St. Paul describes the characteristics of real love: "Love is patient, love is kind. It is not jealous, is not pompous, it is not inflated, it is not rude, it does not seek its own interests, it is not quick-tempered, it does not brood over injury, it does not rejoice over wrongdoing but rejoices with the truth. It bears all things, believes all things, hopes all things, endures all things" (1 Cor 13:4-8). St. Catherine was a shining example of all these characteristics.

As Bishop Barron says, quoting St. Thomas Aquinas, "Love is willing the good of the other as other." Love is an act of the will, not a romantic feeling, and it consciously puts the needs of the beloved first.

4. **St. Catherine spoke often about the blood of Christ; in fact, she repeated the word "blood" over and over moments before her death. What is significant about blood in the Old Covenant? How does blood relate to the New Covenant? (Gen 15:7-12, 17-18; Exod 24:3-8; Lev 17:11; Heb 9:12-14, 22; Luke 22:19-20; CCC 613, 1365)**

Answer: All covenants between God and his people were sealed or confirmed with blood from a sacrifice. In the Old Testament, it was blood from animals that was used to ratify covenants and to atone for sins. God prescribed blood sacrifice for forgiveness of sins: "Blood, as the seat of life, makes atonement." (Lev 17:11, Heb 9:22).

Jesus, as the sacrificial "Lamb of God," poured out his blood on the cross as the sacrifice that ratified the New Covenant once and for all, ending the sacrificial system of the Old Testament. Because of Christ's sacrifice, all sins are forgiven, thus allowing faithful people to be joined with God forever. We re-present this eternal sacrifice of the New Covenant in the sacrament of the Eucharist, where the wine offered becomes the blood of Christ: "This cup which is poured out for you is the New Covenant in my blood" (Luke 22:20).

ST. CATHERINE *of* SIENA
The Mystic
QUESTIONS *for* UNDERSTANDING, PART II

1. **What can the life of St. Catherine show us about God's purpose for us and how we can cooperate with his plan? (Jer 29:11; Ps 139:1-16; CCC 898-900, 1877, 2712, 2724, 2745)**

   Answer: Each of us is created to "show forth the image of God and to be transformed into the image of the Father's only Son" (CCC 1877). God created each of us knowing why he made us and what unique part we have to play in his Kingdom. Each of us has a vocation and is called to model Christ in whatever paths our vocation takes.

   Discerning and following one's vocation requires an active prayer life, which was exhibited by St. Catherine, especially in the area of contemplative prayer. Early in her life, St. Catherine had a vision of Jesus dressed as the pope and surrounded by angels. Shortly thereafter, she became a recluse and devoted herself to constant and contemplative prayer, probably hoping to better understand what this vision meant for her life. Through her prayer, she discerned that she was to remain single, join the lay order of Dominicans, and eventually convince the pope to return to Rome.

   Catherine remained close to Christ through constant prayer, and was directed at each stage in her life by him. It seems she fully cooperated with each path that was shown to her, never shrinking from the direction she was called to follow. God provided all the grace she needed to accomplish her purpose before she was called home to heaven.

2. **How did St. Catherine "witness to a dimension beyond this world" while she was on earth? (CCC 955-957, 2683; Eph 6:10-13)**

   Answer: St. Catherine documented her spiritual visions and communications with Jesus and the saints in her writings. From an early age, she seemed to live each day in the communion of saints, talking about the heavenly realm with the same sense of reality as she spoke about the earthly world.

   We often do not think much about the angels and saints in heaven, so St. Catherine reminds us of their reality and importance. Many of the conflicts and challenges we have during our lives are really spiritual in nature and can only be won through the intervention of heavenly powers, so our connection and reliance on the angels and saints is critical for our spiritual journey here on earth.

3. Define and explain what St. Catherine was referring to when she said, "What is this thing that is ours, given us by God, that neither the devil nor anyone else can take from us?" (Sir 15:11-20; CCC 1730-31)

   Answer: St. Catherine was talking about our will. She also said, "No one can force us to commit the slightest sin, because God has put yes and no into the strongest thing there is, into our will."

   Our will is, in essence, our freedom to make choices during our earthly lives, often between good and evil: "Human freedom is a force for growth and maturity in truth and goodness; it attains its perfection when directed toward God" (CCC 1731).

4. Explain St. Catherine's metaphor about the raging river and the bridge, including the three stages of spiritual growth. (CCC 1852-53; John 14:6; 1 John 4:17-18)

   Answer: The raging river represents the sinful and fallen world, while the bridge represents Jesus Christ as the way to be free from sin and cross safely into eternal life. Our sole hope for salvation is to climb onto the bridge to enter into the divine life of God's only Son, Jesus Christ.

   There are three steps leading up to the bridge of life. The first step, representing most beginners in the spiritual journey, is climbed by the soul desiring to be saved because of his "slavish fear."

   The soul who progresses in faith will next climb the second step, which leads him to reject sin due to his love of God which becomes "holy fear," or fear simply of sinning, not because of personal damnation but because sin is an insult to God. Souls on the second step often love God and neighbor "for their own profit or for the delight and pleasure" found in God.

   To ascend to the third step, souls must, in Catherine's words, "seek perfect knowledge of themselves so that they will know that of themselves they have neither existence nor any grace." In challenging times these souls, in true humility, will seek God alone. As souls persevere in eliminating all slavish fear and selfish desires, they attain to the bridge and walk in true unity with the Trinity in "filial love."

BL. JOHN HENRY NEWMAN
The Convert
QUESTIONS *for* UNDERSTANDING, PART I

1. John Henry Newman's knowledge of Scripture and his study of the writings of the Church Fathers led him to accept Catholicism as the fullness of Christianity. How do Catholic teachings incorporate both Sacred Scripture and Sacred Tradition? (CCC 78-82, 104-05, 133-34, 141)

   Answer: Both are inextricably linked and flow from the same source, the Holy Trinity. Sacred Scripture is the inspired word of God in written form, while Sacred Tradition is that which has been passed down, protected by the Holy Spirit, in oral form through the teaching of his Church. Bishops, as the successors of the apostles, preserve the apostolic teaching in a continuous line until Jesus' second coming.

   "This living transmission, accomplished by the Holy Spirit, is called Tradition. Through Tradition, 'the Church, in her doctrine, life, and worship perpetuates and transmits to every generation all that she herself is, all that she believes'" (CCC 78).

   The Church has always proclaimed the truth of Sacred Scripture and venerated it as "she venerated the Body of the Lord" (CCC 141).

2. How did Newman define the Church from his reading of the Church Fathers? What does this say about the importance of Baptism? (Mark 16:15-16; Matt 28:19-20; CCC 977, 855, 1271)

   Answer: The Church Fathers convinced Newman that the Church is "the communion of those who have received the Holy Spirit through baptism." Although Christians are not fully united, there is only one Christian baptism that unites all believers with Jesus and makes us all "brothers" in God's family. "Baptism therefore constitutes the sacramental bond of unity existing among all who through it are reborn" (CCC 1271).

3. Newman was especially intrigued by the Greek Fathers and their thoughts on the incarnation and the "divinization of the Christian." How is the "divinization of the Christian" to be understood? (John 17:3, 20-23; 2 Pet 1:3-4; 1 John 3:1-2; CCC 460)

   Answer: Christ became man and took on a human nature, so we could share in his divine life for all eternity. The divine and human natures are forever joined in Christ, so if we are "in Christ," we will become partakers of the divine life of the Trinity. We do not become God, but we, as his adopted sons and daughters through Christ, will live in unity with God forever.

4. What does "conversion" mean? Does it happen at one point in time or is it a continual process? Where do we see evidence of Newman's conversion during his life? (Acts 2:38; 2 Cor 5:17; Eph 4:20-24; CCC 1427-28)

Answer: Conversion is an encounter with Christ that leads to repentance for sins and a commitment to live according to God's will. In Second Corinthians, St. Paul says, "whoever is in Christ is a new creation: the old things have passed away; behold new things have come." True conversion is a turning away from our own ego and will to conform more closely to God's will and purpose for our lives.

The *Catechism* explains that the first conversion comes at our initial repentance and acceptance of Jesus as Lord and Savior at our baptism. However, the second conversion is not one point in time but is ongoing throughout our lives as we sin and seek forgiveness.

The first significant moment of Newman's conversion came in adolescence, when he first accepted Christ through the efforts of his Evangelical schoolmaster. The second came when he became Catholic, after having realized that the Church contained the fullness of revealed truth and would bring him closer to Christ.

5. The debate about faith and reason that Newman addressed repeatedly still continues into our times. Relying on Newman's insights, how would you explain that faith and reason are not just compatible but mutually supportive? Give examples of human reason in support of Christian faith. (CCC 154-156, 159)

Answer: Newman believed that there are two types of reasoning: implicit and explicit. He taught that all humans are endowed with implicit reasoning, or the subconscious ability to form conclusions and beliefs from available information and experiences. Implicit reasoning leads to faith in religious and non-religious claims. Explicit reasoning is the conscious discussion or arguments that analyze and reflect on the conclusions of someone's implicit reasoning. Scientific methods fall into the explicit category of reasoning, but exist apart from implicit reasoning. No one can come to faith in *anything* without the innate process of implicit reasoning.

Examples of human reason in support of Christian faith can be: miracles witnessed; prayers answered; logical conclusions about the existence of God from natural revelation; belief in testimony of witnesses to Jesus' death and resurrection; and many others that are as unique as each individual's mind and experiences.

BL. JOHN HENRY NEWMAN

The Convert

QUESTIONS *for* UNDERSTANDING, PART II

1. **Explain Newman's view regarding the development of Christian doctrine over time. How does the Church manage this development and decide what constitutes true and false development? (CCC 890-92, 2034)**

   Answer: Newman argued that Christian doctrines are not given once for all and simply passed down unchanged from generation to generation. Rather, like seeds that unfold into plants or rivers that deepen and broaden over time, their various aspects and implications emerge in the course of time and the engagement of lively minds under the grace of the Holy Spirit. Ideas change because they are living things.

   There are seven criteria Newman presents to determine if the development in the doctrine is legitimate or a corruption. Three of these are:

   - **Preservation of type** - The development preserves the essential form and structure of what came before.
   - **Conservative action upon its past** - Development cannot reverse or contradict what came before
   - **Power of Assimilation** - Taking into the idea what is best for its further development and understanding.

   The teaching office, or Magisterium of the Church, holds the position of final authority on Church doctrine. The Magisterium is made up of the pope and the bishops and acts with infallibility in faith and morals when they "exercise the supreme Magisterium above all in an Ecumenical Council" (CCC 891).

2. **In his book *The Idea of the University*, Newman concluded that universities were in the business of creating gentlemen, and the Church was in the business of creating saints. How does this relate to the universal call to holiness? How does the Catholic Church help its members to grow in holiness and become saints? (1 Pet 1:13-16; 2 Tim 1:9-10; CCC 2013-14, 2813)**

   Answer: All Christians are called to conform their lives to Christ and become like him as adopted sons and daughters of God through him. This is a universal call, not just for a select few, but for all who profess belief in Christianity. Saint Paul said, "He saved us and called us to a holy life, not according to our works but according to his own design and the grace bestowed on us in Christ Jesus" (2 Tim 1:9). God desires an intimate union with his children, and we cannot enter into this union with a sinful nature.

CATHOLICISM: *The Pivotal Players*

17

Grace absolves us of our sin and allows us to progress toward holiness. The Church offers many opportunities to receive grace, first in baptism and then in the other sacraments. Looking to the canonized saints as role models also helps us identify with and better understand lives that are conformed to Christ.

3. In the *Grammar of Assent*, Newman developed his thesis that the key step to faith is *assent*, not *certitude*. Explain the difference between assent and certitude, as well as how they relate to belief in God.

   Answer: Assent is approval or agreement, while certitude is firm knowledge that something is true or correct. Newman believed that coming to *certitude* was not the process that mattered for belief, but that coming to *assent* was more relevant. He saw a big difference between the need to be certain and the quest to understand on some level, which is the basis of assent. We hardly ever get absolute certainty about most things, but we still believe in many of them anyway.

   Coming to assent involves much more than accepting an argument. Newman called the process the "illative sense"—the movement of the mind to the point of assent through formal conclusions based on evidence, and then through informal conclusions based on many other things, such as peer group influence or "truths" passed down from others. We come to assent by an extremely subtle and unconscious process of weighing and accumulating "converging probabilities": my observations and what I've been told always lead me to believe something, even if it's not empirically certain.

   God's existence is not empirically certain. However, Christians believe in him, as they have used their "illative sense" to come to faith.

4. What did Newman think was the most real or concrete evidence for the existence of God? (CCC 1706, 1776, 1778)

   Answer: Newman writes that our conscience gives us concrete access to the reality of God. He calls conscience "a certain, keen sensibility, pleasant or painful, in virtue of which I call certain actions rights or wrong." He refers to conscience as a "voice" that is oriented to something higher than oneself. We are ashamed when we don't follow that voice. Since we can only be ashamed when in front of a person, there must be someone before whom we are responsible.

   Our conscience, if well-formed, is not subjective or based only on opinion. It is God's objective voice within us, guiding our actions to conform to his law and will.

   Thus conscience is a connecting principle between the creature and his Creator; and the firmest hold of theological truths is gained by habits of personal religion. When men begin all their works with the thought of God, acting for his sake, and to fulfill His will, when they ask His blessing on themselves and their life, pray to Him for the objects they desire, and see Him in the event, whether it be according to their prayers or not, they will find everything that happens tends to confirm them in the truths about Him which live in their imagination, varied and unearthly as those truths may be.

5. **Newman suffered much in his life for speaking the truth. What is the core truth of Christianity, and how is sharing this truth the responsibility of all disciples? (John 1:1-5; 8:58; 14:6; CCC 638, 851)**

Answer: The truth of Christianity is that Jesus is the only begotten Son of God, fully human and fully divine. He came into the world to suffer and die as payment for the sins of all. Through his sacrificial death and glorious resurrection, he paid the penalty of sin and defeated death for all mankind, thereby restoring the relationship with God that was broken through original sin.

Through our baptism into the Body of Christ, it is our responsibility to evangelize or share this truth with others, drawing them into a relationship with Christ and with his Church.

G.K. CHESTERTON
The Evangelist
QUESTIONS *for* UNDERSTANDING, PART I

1. Chesterton said that his wife, Frances, was the first Christian he had ever met who was happy. What is happiness or joy? How are they related to faith? (CCC 384, 1718; 1 Pet 1:8-9; John 15:9-12; 16:22; Ps 28:;, 33:21; Prov 16:20; Gal 5:22-23; CCC 1832)

   Answer: Lasting happiness can only come from a deep and abiding relationship with God. This relationship is built on love, hope, and trust. It involves a love for God that is above all other loves, a hope in a future spent in union with God, and trust in God's promises and unconditional love for us.

   Joy is one of the fruits of the Holy Spirit, which are attributes that emanate from a person who is filled with the Holy Spirit through true faith. Joy does not depend on circumstances, but is present deep within our souls through all of life's ups and downs because we are firmly united to the Lord and trust in his care.

2. Humility was one of Chesterton's most notable attributes. What is it and why is it so important to the spiritual life? (Matt 18:1-4; 23:11-12; 5:3; CCC 2546, 2559)

   Answer: Humility can be defined as seeing ourselves as unimportant and having deference to God and to one another. It is the opposite of pride.

   Jesus expects his disciples to be humble and mirror the attitude of a child, who is dependent on adults as we are on God, and the behavior of a servant, who is in the lowest place and works to ensure the good of others. In the beatitudes, Jesus says, "Happy are the poor in spirit," which can be defined as those who practice voluntary humility. Humility is necessary for a fruitful prayer life as we, God's creatures, look to him, the Creator, with an attitude of dependence and submission to his will.

3. How did gratitude lead Chesterton to become a Christian? What are key ways Catholics express gratitude to God? (CCC 1359-60, 1418, 2097; 1 Thess 5:16-18)

   Answer: Through friendships with various writers, Chesterton came to see existence itself as something for which we should be grateful. This gratitude for existence implied gratitude to someone, which he came to believe was what Christians called "God."

   Celebration of the Eucharist, which literally means "thanksgiving," and adoration of the Blessed Sacrament are two ways we Catholics express our gratitude to God for creation, redemption, and sanctification. There are other ways, too, such as simple gratefulness in private prayer and keeping our hearts thankful in all circumstances.

4. **What is a paradox? What are some paradoxes of Christianity? Explain the paradox of the Incarnation and of the Cross. (CCC 517, 525, 616-17)**

    Answer: A paradox, as Bishop Barron says, is the "crashing together of opposites which generates unexpected meaning and insight." It can also be described as a situation, person, or thing that combines apparently contradictory features or qualities.

    There are many paradoxes in Christianity. Some examples include: the first shall be last and the last shall be first; the humble shall be exalted; blessed are the poor; a virgin shall give birth; the dead shall rise; he that lays down his life will gain it; if you give away a gift, you will gain more than you gave; he who loves his life will lose it; Jesus is fully God and fully man; salvation comes through Christ's suffering and death on the cross.

    Paradox of the Incarnation: Jesus is fully God and fully man, one person with two natures. The Creator of the universe and King of all nations takes on a human nature and is born a poor baby in a stable: "In this poverty heaven's glory was made manifest" (CCC 525).

    Paradox of the Cross: Only through Jesus' suffering and death can man attain true happiness and communion with God. A torturous, brutal death of the Son of God is the only way to atone for original and all sin and reunite man with God eternally.

5. **How does Chesterton's Distributism align with Catholic social teaching? (CCC 1928-41, 2425-26)**

    Answer: Chesterton's Distributism is his application of Catholic social teaching, which starts from the same foundation of respect for the dignity of each human being and the rights that flow from this dignity as one of God's creatures. They both emphasize our responsibility to one another and are especially concerned with the disadvantaged members of society.

    Neither Chesterton nor the Church advocate for the dominance of any social institution over and above the individual. Both are against Socialism and support the rightly ordered state. Both call for an equitable distribution of wealth, however, not a distribution unduly imposed by the state, but coming from equitable wages and the charity of all members of a society.

    Chesterton focuses more specifically on the rights of the family and how big government and big business often infringe on those rights by causing both parents to have to work due to low wages, thus separating husband from wife and mother from child. His solution is a more equitable distribution of business ownership, so workers can enjoy the just fruits of their labor and not be utterly dependent on the whims of the rich or the welfare of the state. He advocates for the enlargement of the middle class to reduce the huge gap between the rich and the poor.

G.K. CHESTERTON

The Evangelist

QUESTIONS *for* UNDERSTANDING, PART II

1. **What are the three main themes in Chesterton's writing? How can you use these themes to evangelize? (CCC 905, 2044, 2472, 257, 1730)**

   Answer: Chesterton's main themes include wonder, joy, thankfulness, freedom, and the centrality of God in all things. (Answers to the question of using these themes to evangelize will vary. However, here are some examples:)

   When reaching out to others to share the faith, we should reflect the amazing truth that God loves us and has ordered all of creation to our benefit. People are most attracted to others who are joyful, positive, thankful, and humble.

   Keeping in mind human free will should lead us to *invite* others into a relationship with Jesus Christ and not threaten or coerce them. Explaining the gift of freedom also helps define God as non-competitive and all-loving. It is God's grace that saves, and our efforts are in support of his will. However, each person is free to choose or reject the Gospel.

   Acknowledging God and giving him glory in all circumstances shows our faith. As Chesterton said: "You cannot evade the issue of God. Whether you talk about pigs or the binomial theory, you are still talking about him. If Christianity should happen to be true, then defending it may mean talking about anything or everything. Things can be irrelevant to the proposition that Christianity is false, but nothing can be irrelevant to the proposition that Christianity is true."

2. **What is free will and how is it perfected? (CCC 1730-33, 1738)**

   Answer: Free will is a gift from God to all humankind and is inherent in the dignity of the human person. We are free to initiate and determine our own actions, including the choice for good or evil. Free will attains perfection when it is directed toward God and we choose to put his will above our own. As the *Catechism* states, "The more one does what is good, the freer one becomes and the closer one is to his ultimate good, which is God" (CCC 1731, 1733).

3. **Why is Jesus Christ not "just one religious leader among many"? (John 8:58; 14:6-10; Col 2:9; CCC 469, 653)**

   Answer: Christian faith professes that Jesus is God, the second Person of the Trinity. He is the only religious leader who claimed to be God, which is why he was put to death for blasphemy. Jesus said, "Before Abraham was, I AM," invoking the name God gave Moses at the burning bush. He also told his disciples that if they had seen him, they had seen God, the Father. The truth of Jesus' divinity is confirmed by his resurrection from the dead.

4. **How did Chesterton show that he was a committed disciple of Jesus Christ and a model of lay spirituality in the contemporary world? (CCC 899-900, 1832)**

Answer: Chesterton was a model evangelist. He widely professed his Christian beliefs and his conversion to Catholicism. He never tried to hide his religion or keep it private. On the contrary, he ardently and publically defended Christianity in his writing and speaking. Chesterton took his baptismal responsibility seriously and continually worked to prove the truth of the faith, using his God-given gift of writing.

In addition, he exhibited many fruits of the Holy Spirit: charity, modesty, joy, patience, gentleness, faithfulness, self-control, and chastity.

MICHELANGELO
The Artist
QUESTIONS *for* UNDERSTANDING, PART I

1. **Explain the ban on making images of God that started with the Hebrews. How has the Incarnation affected this perspective? How do holy images, Michelangelo's and others, propagate the faith? (Exod 20:4-5; Deut 4:15-19; Col 1:15; CCC 2129-2132)**

   Answer: A "carved image," as outlawed in the Old Testament, was an idol, often in the form of one of God's creatures (e.g., the golden calf). God forbade worship of anything or anyone other than him, the one true God. Since no one had ever seen God, images of him were impossible to accurately create.

   With the Incarnation, God became man and, as Saint Paul said, was a living image of the invisible God. Worshipping Jesus in his full divinity and humanity is worshipping God. Representations of Christ are not in conflict with the ban on images of idols, as he is the one true God and not a false idol.

   Christian portrayals of Christ are a continuation of the life on earth, in the flesh, of the Word of God. Many people are moved to a deeper faith by sacred art. Also, the truths of the faith can be demonstrated more realistically by paintings, stained glass, and sculpture. However, we need to be careful not to ascribe any supernatural power to those images, or we might end up worshipping the image and not what it represents.

2. **What is the Catholic view of the body? How does Michelangelo's *David* showcase this view? (CCC 364, 369; 1 Cor 15: 42-49; Rom 8:22-23; CCC 991, 997-999; Matt 25:31-46)**

   Answer: The human person is a unity of body and soul, material and spiritual. Both body and soul should be honored and respected, as they both come from God. We are to love the body, as it is a "temple of the Holy Spirit."

   Jesus forever blessed the body by joining it to his divinity. At the Incarnation, Jesus took on a human body, and then he was raised bodily from the dead as the "first fruits of those who have fallen asleep." He did not leave his body behind on earth, but ascended bodily to heaven. Because of Jesus' resurrection and his promise that his disciples would follow him to heaven, Christians profess belief in bodily resurrection for all humankind. At the end of time and before the final judgment, God will raise all from the dead and give them glorified bodies, which we will take into eternal joy or eternal punishment.

   Michelangelo's *David* celebrates the beauty and goodness of the body, which is a "temple of the Holy Spirit," as David and all the faithful are. It gives glory to God as the Creator of such a magnificent creature.

3. **Explain how David relates to and foreshadows Jesus in Scripture. How does Michelangelo's *David* represent this foreshadowing? (1 Sam 17:41-51; 2 Sam 7:1-16; 1 Chron 22:6-10; Matt 1:1; Heb 1:5-9)**

> *Answer:* David was a faithful Israelite, putting God before all others. He conquered the enemy Goliath, as Christ conquered the enemies of Israel (sin and death). David fought for the Lord God, and Jesus came in the name of the Lord as God. David loved the Lord and desired to worship him properly, so he wanted to build a "house" for God where the Ark of the Covenant could reside. Jesus came as the living house, or temple, of God.
>
> The promise God gave to David in Second Samuel through the prophet Nathan is the basis of the Judeo-Christian expectation of a Messiah. God reiterates this covenant with David's son, Solomon, in First Chronicles, promising to establish the royal throne of David in Israel forever. God's promises were fulfilled in Jesus Christ, son of David and Son of God, and the everlasting Kingdom of God was inaugurated with the Incarnation.
>
> Michelangelo captured the purity, piety, and determination of David in the face and posture of his sculpture. He is not depicted as a vacant, mythological figure, like the *Apollo Belvedere*, but as a man made in the image and likeness of God. Bishop Barron says that Christ is the "realization of what God has always intended for humanity," and this is portrayed by the perfect form of the *David*.

4. **What does the *Pietà* communicate about Mary and Jesus in terms of their relationship? What is communicated about the Eucharist? (CCC 964, 1391)**

> *Answer:* The *Pietà* shows a strong family relationship between Jesus and Mary, as their facial features are almost identical. Mary is depicted as forever young in her eternal, mystical role as spouse, mother, and daughter of God. She is humanly and supernaturally connected to Christ and suffers with him, in him, and through him.
>
> Mary, our Mother, gave Christ to us by her "Yes" to God at the Annunciation, and the *Pietà* shows her continuing to give Christ to us after his death. Her left hand is extended, giving Jesus to the world; her right hand is pressing him close, but through the veil of her garment, just as the priest shows Christ to us when he lifts the monstrance holding the Blessed Sacrament. In the *Pietà*, Mary also represents the Church, as she offers us the body and blood, soul and divinity of her Son in the Eucharist.

5. **How is the Church our *Mater et Magistra* (*Mother and Teacher*)? (Eph 5:25-28, 32; Rev 21:9-11; CCC 507, 2040, 2047; Matt 28:18-20, 1 Tim 3:15; 1 Cor2:12-13; CCC 2032-34, 2037-38)**

> *Answer:* The Church is our mother for many reasons. First of all, she is the "bride of Christ," whom he loves and calls his own body. She produces children through preaching and the sacrament of baptism. Our mother, the Church, feeds us with the word of God and with the Body and Blood of her Son. She grants the mercy of God, especially in the sacrament

of reconciliation. Christian life finds its nourishment in the liturgy and the celebration of the sacraments (CCC 2047).

Right before he ascended to heaven, Jesus commanded his disciples, the brand new Church, to teach all the nations "to observe all that I have commanded you." Thus, the Church has been entrusted with the law of God. Through the inspiration and gifts of the Holy Spirit, she preserves and preaches the law of God. The principle teaching office of the Church is the Magisterium, which consists of the pope and all the bishops. Others in the Church teach the faith as well: theologians, spiritual authors, priests, teachers, and catechists. In fact, according to the *Catechism*, each practicing Christian is called to teach the commandments of Christ: "Faith and the practice of the Gospel provide each person with an experience of 'life in Christ,' who enlightens him and makes him able to evaluate the divine and human realities according to the Spirit of God" (CCC 2038).

MICHELANGELO
The Artist
QUESTIONS *for* UNDERSTANDING, PART II

1. **Not much is known about Michelangelo's interior life. What can we learn about his faith based on his works? (Matt 7:15-20; CCC 901, 1704)**

   Answer: You can evaluate a tree by the fruit it bears and a prophet by the life he or she leads and the works he or she produces. With this advice from Jesus, we can look at Michelangelo's artistic output and see visible signs of his interior faith. While only the Lord can judge our hearts, the genius, magnificence, and truth of Michelangelo's works attest to the Holy Spirit working through him.

2. **Explain what Bishop Barron means when he says that creation was an "act of division and God continues to separate." (Gen 1:1-10; 2:21-23; Lev 20:26; Luke 11:23; 12:51-53; Matt 25:31-43)**

   Answer: In the beginning, God created the world and even a companion for the first man through successive acts of separation: darkness from light, earth from sky, land from sea, woman from man's rib. Then God set Israel apart from other nations to be his own, to be the nation that would produce our Messiah and Savior.

   Like those of many prophets before him, Jesus' words and actions necessitate a choice to align with God or go our own way. Prophetic action always disturbs the peace of our self-complacency. Jesus continues his Father's acts of separation and division by his very existence, as each person must choose to follow him or not.

   At the end of time, Jesus will come to judge all people, separating the saved from the damned, thus completing what was begun at creation.

3. **In the center panel of the Sistine Chapel ceiling, what truth about the creation of man is represented by God's pointing finger? (Gen 2:7; CCC 33, 362, 366)**

   Answer: According to Genesis, God created man's physical form out of the "clay of the ground" and then breathed life into him. Michelangelo represents this breath of divine energy or life as God's pointing finger. More specifically, the action of God's pointing finger represents the creation of man's eternal soul in the image and likeness of God. Bishop Barron comments that this detail depicts the transmission of the eternal *logos*, or "mind" (reason), of God to man.

4. **Explain how Noah's ark represents the Church. (Gen 6:11-14; 7:1; 1 Pet 3:18-22; CCC 845, 1180)**

   Answer: God was displeased with humanity and planned to send a flood to destroy everyone, except Noah and his family, whom he judged as righteous. God instructed Noah to build an ark to save them from death during the flood. Saint Peter says that Noah's ark saved eight persons "through water," which prefigured baptism. Through the sacrament of baptism, given by the Church, we are cleansed of all sin and united with Christ, thereby saving us from eternal death. Church Fathers, such as Saint Augustine and Saint Ambrose, were fond of using a boat as a metaphor for the Church, the place where humanity is called together to become the "world reconciled" to God. They also spoke of the Church as being prefigured by "Noah's ark, which alone saves from the flood."

5. **Explain how Mary represents the Ark of the New Covenant. How does Jesus embody the three things that were carried in the original Ark of the Covenant? (Exod 25:8-16; Rev 11:19-12:1-2; CCC 2676; Heb 9:3-4; Mt 5:17-19; Jn 6:48-51; 1 Chron 23:13; Heb 5:1-6)**

   Answer: Mary held Jesus Christ, the New Covenant, in her womb. So she is the tabernacle, or the ark, of the New Covenant. The original Ark of the Covenant was the dwelling place of God in the Holy of Holies for the Israelites as they wandered forty years in the desert. It held three things central to the Old Covenant: the tablets of the Ten Commandments; manna that fed the wandering Israelites; and the staff of the high priest, Aaron. All three things are given to us in the person of Jesus Christ through the New Covenant: the law has come to fulfillment in Christ; we are fed with his own body and blood and receive everlasting life; and Jesus is the eternal high priest.

6. **Michelangelo placed his Jonah depiction in the Sistine Chapel right above *The Last Judgment*. Why could Jonah be so closely associated with the resurrection of the dead? (Jon 2:1, 11; 3:1-5; Matt 12:38-42)**

   Answer: When the Pharisees asked for a miraculous sign of Jesus' power, he responded that no sign would be given except for the sign of Jonah. Jonah was in the belly of the whale for three days, where he should have died, just as Jesus was in the tomb for three days after his death. Both were "resurrected" by God's power to fulfill a divine plan. Jonah finally obeyed God and went to Nineveh to preach repentance, and Jesus was "obedient unto death," and so eternal life is possible for all who repent and follow him.

7. **How is Christianity the "greatest humanism possible," as Bishop Barron states? (CCC 460-63)**

   Answer: Christianity is the only religion that claims that the one true God became man and dwelt among us. There is no greater love expressed for humanity than the love that would propel the eternal God and Creator of the universe to join a human nature to his own. The act of the Incarnation elevates humanity to a godly status, unparalleled in any other version of man's history and destiny. Through Christ, in him, and with him we all become participants in the divine life.